Finding Jesus,
Discovering Self

Praise for *Finding Jesus, Discovering Self*

"Goldman and Dols offer more than a sensitive understanding of the Jew from Nazareth; they offer a courageous, poetic, and profound understanding of humanity's brokenness and isolation, and our potentials for healing and wholeness." —Amy-Jill Levine, E. Rhodes and Leona B. Carpenter Professor of New Testament Studies, Vanderbilt University Divinity School and Graduate Department of Religion

"William Dols and Caren Goldman offer us space, warmth, and nourishment. The authors highlight key stories in the life of Jesus by drawing upon their own candid autobiographies, skillfully posed questions linked with imaginative exercises, and artfully chosen readings." —Robert Owens Scott, Director Trinity Institute & Founding Editor *Spirituality And Health* magazine

"[*Finding Jesus, Discovering Self*] allows me as a Jewish reader to learn from the life of a great spiritual leader who has been historically off-limits to Jews." —Rabbi Bruce Bromberg Seltzer, Chaplain, Smith College; Religious Advisor, Amherst College; and Director, Smith/Amherst Hillel

"William Dols and Caren Goldman give diverse communities of faith a remarkable new way of encountering the Jesus of the scriptures. An invaluable resource to those of us working in multi-faith contexts." —Jennifer L. Walters, Dean of Religious Life, Smith College, Northampton, Massachusetts

"Drawing on the insights of humanism and depth psychology, the authors give us the tools we need to explore the archetypal meanings of sacred scripture and to find and embrace the questions that can change our lives." —Margaret Bullitt-Jonas, author of *Holy Hunger* and *Christ's Passion, Our Passions*

"*Finding Jesus, Discovering Self* offers a remarkably rich, authentic, and inspiring way to work (and walk) with the stories of Jesus. Its combining of the gospel narratives with fearless inquiry, strong confessional voices, and resonant amplifications from poetry, literature, and film speaks to the heart and demonstrates the breadth of the Holy Spirit." —E. H. Rick Jarow, Associate Professor of Religion, Vassar College

"Walks you through the biblical story and helps you to see your own likeness in it. Whether you're trying to find your voice, licking your wounds, or just trying to make the next decision about how to live your life, this is the book to help you live into that likeness." —Ana Hernandez, author of *The Sacred Art of Chant*

"Blend together the Wisdom of Jesus, the psychological insights of Carl Jung, the integration of Elizabeth Boyden Howes, and the lively experience of the authors and the results are the book in your hands." —John Beverley Butcher, author of *The Tao of Jesus* and *Telling the Untold Stories*

"Not only worthwhile reading for our time, but an inspiration for those who choose to walk the path of spiritual awakening and risk living into the questions of Jesus." —Carolyn Craft, Executive Director of WISDOM Radio and host of WISDOM Radio's "Inner WISDOM"

"An ideal companion: clear, compassionate, celebratory, and unique." —Nina Frost, president of The Vocare Group and author of *Soul Mapping*

"Profound in its psychological and spiritual insight and full of compelling human stories, this book offers a wealth of reflections and penetrating questions to last a lifetime." —Rev. D. Andrew Kille, PhD, director of Interfaith Space and author of *Psychological Biblical Criticism*

"An autobiographical exegesis that is capable of transforming those who participate in it. I could scarcely put it down." —Dr. Walter Wink, Professor of Biblical Interpretation, Auburn Theological Seminary

CAREN GOLDMAN and WILLIAM DOLS

Finding Jesus,
Discovering Self

passages to healing and wholeness

MOREHOUSE PUBLISHING
HARRISBURG PENNSYLVANIA

Unless otherwise noted, the Scripture quotations contained herein are from the New Revised Standard Version Bible, copyright © 1989 by the Division of Christian Education of the National Council of Churches of Christ in the U.S.A. Used by permission. All rights reserved.

Morehouse Publishing, P.O. Box 1321, Harrisburg, PA 17105

Morehouse Publishing, 445 Fifth Avenue, New York, NY 10016

Morehouse Publishing is an imprint of Church Publishing Incorporated.

Cover design by Corey Kent

Page design by Beth Oberholtzer

Library of Congress Cataloging-in-Publication Data

Goldman, Caren.
    Finding Jesus, discovering self : passages to healing and wholeness / Caren Goldman and William Dols.
        p.   cm.
    Includes index.
    ISBN-13: 978-0-8192-2199-5 (pbk.)
    1. Jesus Christ—Meditations.   2. Bible. N.T. Gospels—Meditations.
I. Dols, William L. (William Ludwig), 1933–   II. Title.
BT306.43.G65   2006
232—dc22

                                                              2005027889

Printed in the United States of America

    06   07   08   09   10   11   6   5   4   3   2

When your children ask you
in time
to come...

—Deuteronomy 6:20

Wesley	Jax
Carter	Andie
Jennifer	Evan
Katherine	Chris
	Jamie
	Trace

CONTENTS

About the Authors   viii
Acknowledgments   x
Foreword by Robert Scott   xi
Introduction   xiii
Suggestions for Using This Book   xix

1. Leaving Home   1
2. Beginning the Journey   8
3. Living with Wilderness   15
4. Returning Home   25
5. Weathering Storms   33
6. Speaking One's Truth   40
7. Loving with All   47
8. Standing Up Straight   54
9. Binding Wounds   61
10. Crossing Boundaries   70
11. Choosing Life   80
12. Discovering God's Kingdom   87
13. Entering the Heart of the Matter   96
14. Betraying Trust   103
15. Epilogue: Breeding New Algebras   112

Endpapers   121
Notes   129
Resources   133
Bibliography   139
Permissions   145
Index   147

ABOUT THE AUTHORS

Caren Goldman, a Jewish author and award-winning journalist, specializes in writing about spirituality, health, religion, and the arts and humanities. She is the author of *Healing Words for the Body, Mind, and Spirit: 101 Words to Inspire and Affirm* (Marlowe & Co.) and the writer of *Vitality and Wellness: An Omega Institute Mind, Body, Spirit Book* (Dell), an associate editor of *The Bible Workbench*, and a former associate editor of the *Cleveland Jewish News*. For over thirty years, hundreds of her freelance articles about the intersections of spirituality, health, and religion have appeared in national magazines including *Spirituality and Health*, *Coping*, *Forward Day-by-Day*, *New Age Journal*, *Natural Health*, *Yoga Journal*, and *Intuition*, as well as major metropolitan daily and weekly newspapers. In the late 1990s, a *Washington Post* review of magazines focusing on spirituality and health singled out Caren's exceptional writing about those subjects.

Caren began her writing career as a news and features reporter at the *Cleveland Plain Dealer*. She also leads seminars and retreats throughout the country and works as a Bridgebuilder conflict resolution consultant to congregations and nonprofit organizations. Caren is listed in Who's Who of American Women 2006 and she also plays an accordion to amaze and amuse—mostly herself. She and her husband, Ted Voorhees, live in Massachusetts and West Virginia. Caren can be contacted by e-mail at words forhealing@aol.com or via her website: www.carengoldman.com.

William L. Dols is an ordained Episcopal priest with a PhD in biblical studies and psychology from the Graduate Theological Union and the University of California. As a parish priest Bill served congregations in Maryland,

Virginia, and North Carolina for twenty-five years before returning to graduate school full-time. Afterwards, he spent eight years as executive director of the Educational Center, a nonprofit organization that, since 1945, has provided resources and training designed to equip people of all ages and institutions worldwide to become interpreters of life who are able to decipher the meaning of their own experience.

Bill is the author of *Three-Dimensional Man* (privately published), *Awakening the Fire Within* (The Educational Center), and *Just Because It Didn't Happen* (Myers Park Baptist Church). Fifteen years ago, while leading the Educational Center in new directions, Bill created *The Bible Workbench*, a biblical resource that he continues to edit. *The Bible Workbench* is used nationwide by individuals and groups for Bible study and by clergy for weekly sermons. In 1995, Bill returned to parish ministry for six years as minister of education at the Myers Park Baptist Church in Charlotte, North Carolina.

Parker Palmer, author of *Let Your Life Speak* and *The Courage to Teach*, writes: "For many years, Bill Dols has been reclaiming the treasures of Christian tradition in ways that speak to contemporary seekers, while preserving the mystery and magnificence of the truth at the heart of Christian faith. In a time like ours—so thirsty for wisdom but so resistant to traditional formulations—his voice is very important. He is a man who has wrestled faithfully with our deepest questions of meaning, and who speaks openly, honestly, and powerfully about fear and faith and all that lies between."

Nationally known for his outstanding preaching and lectures, Bill also leads seminars, retreats, and workshops for congregations of all denominations as well as non-church groups. He and his wife, Shirley, live in Alexandria, Virginia, and have two daughters and two grandsons. Bill can be contacted by e-mail at Wdols@aol.com.

ACKNOWLEDGMENTS

To begin at the beginning would be to go back five years and thank a list of peers and friends, spouses and each other for pokes, prods, and reassuring words that this book could and should be. But we won't begin by going there. Instead, we begin by thanking our editor, Nancy Fitzgerald, a woman of courage and vision as well as a talented and trustworthy shepherd. From the time we first spoke and she said, "Yes!" Nancy brought so much more to this project than a mere stamp of approval. Today, she continues to do so as not only our editor, but our friend.

Without the encouragement and mentoring of the founding mothers of the Guild For Psychological Studies in San Francisco—Elizabeth Boyden Howes, Sheila Moon, and Luella Sibbald—we both know our lives would have been very different and this book would never be. Their unwavering dedication to living the questions of a first-century Jew named Jesus of Nazareth and their invitation to others to forsake answers and consider a similar path is the very heart and soul of this book.

It is a path that has led through the Educational Center in St. Louis where for fifteen years people like Ann Baker and Sara McDonald have enabled *The Bible Workbench* to become part of spiritual journeys in countless groups within the walls and well outside of places called "church." The musings and questions in "Wonderings and Wanderings" will sound familiar to friends in Charlotte and Toledo as well as those who in seminars and workshops across the country have taught us how to be what Keats called "priests of the imagination."

As for so many others, especially Shirley and Ted, who inspired, taught, helped, pushed, challenged, tolerated and loved us along the way, we express our heartfelt gratitude to all of you. For whom you have been and who you are on your never-ending journeys to find Jesus and discover self as a passage to healing and wholeness is, indeed, a blessing.

FOREWORD

Invitations come in many forms. They arrive constantly. Our challenge and our
pleasure lie in deciding which to accept.

The book you are now holding invites you to make fresh discoveries about
the two people named in the title: Jesus and yourself. Now, we know that
invitations to "meet Jesus" aren't always welcome. They often seem to mean
"become like me" and are issued by someone we would prefer not to
become like, thank you very much, someone who claims to have life all figured out and to be filled with supernatural assurance—if only the white
knuckles clutching life's armchair didn't put the lie to that assertion. And
what about the other character in the title: yourself? Bookstore shelves groan
under the weight of (would-be) self-help books that dissolve into puddles of
narcissism. The invitation to discover yet another program for what Thomas
Moore, author of the genuinely helpful *Care of the Soul*, likes to call "the
project to be perfect" (not a venture he recommends) arrives with a thud.

I'm happy to report that this book is neither of those things. I mention
them at the outset for the same reason a sculptor starts with a block of stone
to arrive at a statue: by chipping away what something isn't, you reveal the
contours of what it is. It's an especially helpful technique when, like this
book, the thing you're describing doesn't easily fit preexisting categories.

What you will discover if you accept the invitation to delve into this
remarkable book is neither an imposition nor a curriculum but an authentic welcome issued in the spirit of true hospitality. William Dols and Caren
Goldman offer us space, warmth, and nourishment. They graciously allow
each of us to partake according to our need and our hunger.

Rather than beginning with a stained-glass Jesus or a pat therapeutic
model of "self," the authors create an open yet coherent montage, out of
which different pictures will emerge for each reader. Chapter by chapter,
as the authors highlight key stories in the life of Jesus, they draw upon

their own candid autobiographies, skillfully posed questions linked with imaginative exercises (born of their long experience as workshop leaders), and artfully chosen readings. All of these become means to encounter both Jesus and self in fresh, life-enhancing ways.

In their "Reflections," Dols and Goldman hold back none of their own struggles, mistakes, breakthroughs, and joys, thereby inviting each of us to mine our own stories for the gifts buried within. In "Wonderings and Wanderings," they offer simple tools that allow us to enter into the unfolding story through thought and imagination. And in "Mirrors" they hold up a series of apt but pleasantly unexpected bits of prose and poetry in which we can find our own deepest thoughts and experiences reflected, affirmed, and enlarged.

As practitioners of radical hospitality, the authors require no qualifications for entry. Whatever you know or believe about Jesus—or, for that matter, about yourself—is the perfect place to start: your love, your questions, even your anger. The authors wisely and generously lay out their own assumptions about Jesus right up front, freeing us from the need to read between those particular lines.

In Dols's and Goldman's good company, we come to realize how many invitations have been arriving in our lives without our recognizing them. It isn't too much of a stretch to view our joys as invitations to know ourselves better. But what about the times we screw up? Our broken relationships? That sinking feeling that we've taken a wrong turn and have wound up in a desolate place? Viewed with compassion and mediated by our willingness to live the questions, our weak points become spots where new life, authentic hope, and greater joy can enter. The areas where life wears us down reveal themselves to be the proverbial "thin places" where we sense the divine shimmering within the mundane.

Finally, though, I have to admit that this book is not for everybody. If your life has unfolded without struggle, every relationship has been one of mutual fulfillment, and your ego has never risen to fight a bloody battle against your reality, you can probably pass this invitation by. This book would make no sense to you. But then, neither would the Bible. For the rest of us, however, Dols and Goldman offer a golden opportunity to attend to our deepest yearnings, expressed in the life of Jesus and the lives of each one of us. It's an invitation I hope you'll accept.

Robert Owens Scott
Director, Trinity Institute
Founding Editor, *Spirituality and Health*
New York

INTRODUCTION

As you read the pages ahead, you will see that the stories in this book are about Jesus of Nazareth. If you were not raised Christian or if you are one who feels exiled from your Christian roots, your reaction may be to put it back on the store shelf. We ask that you hold off doing that and read on.

Perhaps the most important thing we can tell you about *Finding Jesus, Discovering Self* is that we wrote it for everyone—no matter what your religious and spiritual beliefs are now or what your lack of them has been. Certainly, for some of you, the stories we've chosen may be like family stories—so familiar because you grew up hearing them as part of a Christian upbringing. If so, we now invite you to set aside temporarily any reading glasses that use creeds, catechisms, and confessions to filter Jesus' life, and to give yourself permission to experience these ancient stories as though you were meeting them for the very first time.

For others—those who may have followed or now follow different spiritual paths, other wisdom-keepers, or no path in particular—this may be your first encounter with a man whose life, death, and relationship to the Divine influenced the course of history in unique and profound ways. If so, we invite you, too, to put any conventional wisdom or prior convictions you may have about Jesus aside for a bit and enter into the stories that follow with open eyes and ears.

Throughout this book, we do not intend or hope to change your beliefs about Jesus or to foist any of ours upon you. In fact, if we've done our job well, by the time you finish *Finding Jesus, Discovering Self*, you will still wonder what either of us may or may not believe about Jesus, with these exceptions:

- A Jewish man named Jesus lived and died in the early years of the Common Era.
- Christ was not his family name.
- He was born and died a Jew.
- To understand him one must look at his life in the context of first-century Judaism and the Roman occupation of his homeland.
- He did not found a church or *the* Church, but went to synagogues.
- After Jesus died, Jews were killed in his name.
- Gospel accounts of his personal life and ministry differ radically in many places.

Ultimately, we hope to introduce you to a process that can engage your mind as well as your senses to help you see these and other stories from ancient traditions as mirrors of what may be happening in the world around you and in your life. This process can empower you to do the following:

- Begin living those difficult, easy-to-avoid questions you have about yourself, your relationships, your job, your links to the society in which you live, and anything else that impacts your private and public worlds.
- View the real world around you, as well as the one reported in newspapers and magazines or on the nightly news or the Internet, from fresh perspectives.
- Awaken and give voice to your body's deep-seated wisdom through the suggested use of art materials (pens, pencils, crayons, paints, markers, clay, found objects), music, body movement, journaling, film, contemporary readings, and other media.
- Discover new ways to make healthy, mature, creative, and life-affirming choices that can help you move forward on your unique journey to healing and wholeness.

Not too long ago, Caren's granddaughter Andie watched the movie *The Prince of Egypt*, which retells the story of Moses' encounter with his God and subsequent quest to set the enslaved Israelites free. When it ended, Andie, then eight, asked, "Is this story true? Did it really happen, or is it a myth?"

Did it really happen, or is it a myth? "Just because it didn't happen doesn't mean it isn't true." When we lead seminars and workshops, we often use that line attributed to novelist Tim O'Brien, because his words remind us that the determining question in addressing a story is not so much *if* or *how* it happened, but *whether* it might be true. In the ancient past, throughout the sacred texts that Jewish people call the Bible and others refer to as the Old Testament, the chroniclers seemed intent not so much on literal reportage and factual biography as on telling and recording stories true to experiences born of an important relationship or revelation. In turn, these stories became vehicles for individuals and communities to reflect on universal meanings and create cultural identities.

Back then, the operative question that arose from such stories about Jesus was not so much whether or not they happened in a particular way as what truth might be brought forth out of the experience a writer or community of writers had with Jesus and his followers. What occurred at the intersection of the God of the Jews and themselves? What, today, might these writers still want me to know about their individual and collective experiences of the Holy?

Today, we call true stories that have never happened, such as those about the hero's journey, *archetypal*. As such, they are timeless accounts, narratives, legends, fairy tales, myths, tall tales, folktales, and yarns that not only arrest our attention and captivate our imagination, but also reflect basic and underlying patterns of life that harbor eternal truths about humankind and the human condition. Eternal truths hidden in each of our psyches and souls patiently wait to emerge and speak.

In the stories that follow about Jesus, we encourage you to taste-test some of those truths by moving the question "What does this text mean?" to one side of your plate to make room for new questions that ask: How do I experience this story in my life, in this time, and in this place? How is this story an event in my family, my community, and the world around me? How does it occur around me, between you and me, and within me? How do these stories act as vehicles that carry my longings, desires, and projections upon others—and even Jesus—out of the psychic realm and into the world? How might this story and the multimedia experiential offerings in this book connect me to those parts of my body, psyche, and soul that I may have forgotten, denied, or repressed? How does this story help me to remember events that assure me a place in the history of humankind, and to *re*-member—to reintegrate—those rejected, unforgiven, and wounded parts of me that yearn to come home so I can drink from the wellsprings of healing, hope, and wholeness that they offer?

Indeed, when we choose to liberate Bible stories from their ecclesiastical Egypt—that remote place of exile—in which solemn assemblies have enslaved them, we can look at a prince of Egypt named Moses, or the son of an unmarried woman named Mary, with the wide-open, wonder-filled eyes of a child and re-vision others' truths into our own. And in so doing, we may discover that no matter how many times we read these stories, they will essentially remain the same. However, we will not. Moreover, as the mystery of their multiple meanings dwells from one stage of life to another in our hearts, minds, and spirits, we encounter moments when suddenly, and perhaps unexpectedly, the stories are born and reborn anew within and between us.

In *Beyond Belief*, Elaine Pagels recalls Christmas Eve at the Church of the Heavenly Rest in New York City and writes of how in "the sounds and the silence, the candlelight and darkness, I felt the celebration take us in and break over us like the sea. . . . For a moment I was shocked by the thought: We could have made all this up out of what had happened in our lives; but, of course, we did not *have* to do that, for, as I realized at once, countless *other* people have already done that, and have woven the stories of innumerable lives into the stories and music, the meanings and visions of Jesus' birth."[1]

Pagels notes that Irenaeus (200 CE), a church father and an adversary of heresy[2] as the early church moved toward forming an official belief with a creed, "thought it heresy to assume that human experience is analogous to divine reality, and to infer that each one of us, by exploring our own experience, may discover intimations of truth about God."[3]

What Irenaeus called "heresy" is precisely what we are doing in this book. We are assuming that within and between us we are living out biblical stories that, when informed by our own experience, do indeed lead to intimations of eternal truths about God, Jesus, and us.

In her novel *By the Light of My Father's Smile*, master storyteller Alice Walker describes Susannah's visit to Irene, the mysterious dwarf she meets in Greece. One day Irene does the Tarot, an ancient storytelling and revelatory instrument with the characters appearing on cards, for Susannah:

> Irene took up the card with a woman and a man entering an ancient carriage. The man's hand under the woman's elbow. She placed the card alongside her nose and closed her eyes, it seemed to Susannah, carefully. She rested a moment, deep in thought.
>
> "Do you know why there is this concept of 'ladies first'?" asked Irene. "It is because, in the early days, if we were permitted to walk behind the man, we would run away. If we were kept in front, they could keep an eye on us. Later on, as we became more tame, they hated to think a woman they desired would only think of running away, and so they invented chivalry, gallantry, the lifting over puddles, the handing into carriages."

"Yes," said Susannah, "but what does this mean aside from that?"

"There is a man inside you, your own inner man, so to speak, and he is dedicated to helping you. He is lifting you into the carriage of your own body, in which you can begin to take charge of your own life."

"Who could that be?" thought Susannah.

"It is not someone of whom you would think," said Irene, as if over-hearing her thoughts. "Besides, it is an inner man, part of yourself. But there is an outer man as well, who calls this inner helper forth.

"I see here," said Irene, holding a card of a woman riding the moon, "that you have been far away. You have been lost, really. You have enjoyed being lost, in a way. Being lost means no one knows where to find you. If no one knows where to find you, then you are safe from expectations. In a word, free. That is what being lost sometimes means. But now, it is as if you are calling to yourself, 'Susannah, Susannah, come back; come home.'" Irene chuckled. "And a little child-woman, far away, sitting I think in a large tree, hears the calling and thinks, Maybe it is time to go back."[4]

Within each of us also lives one who is lost and enjoys being lost, free thereby to avoid and deny and to feel detached from others' expectations of who we will become. This person inside of us is the one who gets lost in dark and devious ways that hurt and bruise, or in bright and honored ways, doing some of the best things people ever do.

Being lost happens not only in wilderness places, but also in executive suites and schools and even in the arms of those who love us the most and for whom we would lay down our lives. Throughout the ages, philosophers, poets, and authors have written about the terrifying possibility of being able, which is, we suspect, what induces—and indeed seduces—many of us to remain satisfied with staying lost. By example, stories about Jesus teach us about letting go, being lost, embracing the terrifying possibility of being able, and coming home. Said another way, stories about Jesus beckon us to hear the call from the tree where we once hid a long, long time ago and choose to come back to self, to others, and even to God. In the world of story, those whom Jesus encounters—the bent-over woman, the blind beggar, the hemorrhaging woman, and the lost son or daughter whom we each are—may finally risk standing up straight, speaking one's truth, seeing the world with new eyes, going home, and at last, choosing to say, "Yes!"

SUGGESTIONS FOR
USING THIS BOOK

Be assured there is no "right" or "wrong" way to use this book. Our goal is to invite and encourage you to go on a unique journey to *live* questions about the life of Jesus, the questions posed by Jesus, the world around you, and your own life:

- by staying in the center of opposing forces that pull you in opposite directions and toward predictable answers, so that the tension you feel can stimulate new thoughts, insights, and feelings about the text, the questions, and your foregone conclusions about the text;
- not feeling that you ever have to have answers to the questions raised in this book;
- and by accepting that premise you may change your mind about what you read, experience, believe, and conclude at any time.

Like all books, this one has a beginning beyond the introduction. In this case, the poem "Sometimes" by David Whyte before the first chapter acts as a doorway to the rest of the book. Stepping through will help to ground you in our open-ended approach to the texts in each of the chapters. Although we suggest you move on chapter by chapter once through the doorway, we designed the book so that you can also wander where your curiosity and intuition guide you.

Don't feel that you have to take in everything a chapter offers at one time. The different sections contribute to the whole in numerous ways. For example, every chapter begins with a passage from a gospel by Mark, Matthew, or Luke. A personal reflection by either Caren or Bill follows.

Hopefully, the questions and exercises in "Wanderings and Wonderings" will generate new ways for you to ponder the passage. A final section titled "Mirrors" completes each chapter. This section contains quotes, poetry, fiction, and nonfiction that can help to expand the gospel passage, the Reflections, and the Wanderings and Wonderings.

Although many of you will approach the fifteen chapters in a linear way, others will find it best to follow their own road map throughout the book, perhaps by reading the introduction and then skipping straight to whatever chapter calls or interests them. Some of you may read each chapter by beginning with the passage about Jesus and then moving on to the Reflection, Wanderings and Wonderings, and then Mirrors. However, others will find a different path. As we mentioned earlier, there is no right or wrong way to find a first-century Jew named Jesus and live his questions between the covers of this book. You get the idea.

We believe that poet and physician William Carlos Williams captured an important value of the experiential offerings in *Finding Jesus, Discovering Self* when he wrote, "There is neither beginning nor end to the imagination but it delights in its own seasons reversing the usual order at will." As mentioned earlier, we designed the exercises to help you engage your imagination to experience the stories about Jesus holistically—not just in your head, but in your body, too. While some of you will have attended retreats and workshops where visualization, music, art materials, mime, and movement helped to awaken other senses and ways of knowing "left brain" material, for others this may be the first time you are being asked to try doing so. If you feel awkward about entering these waters, know you are not alone. To help you take your first steps beyond those feelings, concerns, and even fears, we suggest the following:

- Do what feels comfortable and let the rest go. You can always return to the other activities and suggestions later.
- Ask yourself where the resistance may be coming from. Could it be, perhaps, a prior judgment, an old tape playing in your head, a feeling of awkwardness, or some other source?
- Play soft, slow music without lyrics, such as Pachabel's Canon in D, Bach's Air on a G String, and similar pieces by Mozart, other classical composers, and your favorite contemporary recording artists.
- None of the exercises in this book will ask you to draw a picture. Instead, several ask that you "express" your thoughts, feelings, and responses to parts of a story by using art materials. For some of you this may mean just putting a pencil line or a scribble on a piece of

paper. For others it may mean using different media to make two- or three-dimensional expressions. Keep "art" materials such as paper, pencils, crayons, markers, watercolors, clay, old magazines, or whatever additional media appeals to you nearby.

• The bibliography will point you in the direction of scholarly information about Jesus and his times as well as relevant contemporary writings about healing the mind, body, and spirit.

Finally, because *Finding Jesus, Discovering Self* invites you to become a probing detective uncovering multiple layers of meaning in the biblical texts, we include a section with a suggested film for each chapter. Of course, the value of these films to expand your questions and conclusions about the text will depend on your unique perspective. So if this is your first venture into exploring the "reel" power of film to mirror biblical stories, start by viewing the ones listed. Remember, just because it didn't happen doesn't mean it isn't true—on the screen, on the page, in the world around you, or in your heart and soul.

Sometimes
by David Whyte[5]

Sometimes
if you move carefully
through the forest

breathing
like the ones
in the old stories

who could cross
a shimmering bed of dry leaves
without a sound,

you come
to a place
whose only task

is to trouble you
with tiny
but frightening requests

conceived out of nowhere
but in this place
beginning to lead everywhere.

Requests to stop what
you are doing right now,
and

to stop what you
are becoming
while you do it,

questions
that can make
or unmake
a life,

questions
that have patiently
waited for you,

questions
that have no right
to go away.

ONE

LEAVING HOME

In those days Jesus came from Nazareth of Galilee and was baptized by John in the Jordan. (Mark 1:9)

Reflections
BY CAREN

Not long ago, my husband, Ted, and I sat on piles of boxes we had just packed and wondered how many different ways we would or could say "Good-bye" to fifteen years of life in Toledo, Ohio, before saying "Hello" to a new job and other beginnings that awaited us in Northampton, Massachusetts. Smiling, Ted recalled that we originally planned to stay in Toledo only two years, but hour by hour, day by day, and eventually year by year we marked an additional thirteen off our calendars.

For us, the rust belt city of Toledo was only to be a stopping-off point where we would begin our relationship as husband and wife, advance our careers, and make plans to "get out of Dodge" and go to some unknown place. In retrospect, life in three different houses in Toledo became all of that. But it also became something we never imagined. It also became *home*.

Thomas Wolfe's heart-wrenching conclusion that "you can't go home again" assumes that for all of us naming that which we call home and then leaving it is one of life's defining moments. The decision to stay home or leave home reminds us that one of the blessings and the curses of having free will and being a choice maker is that there will always be roads not taken in our lives.

Most obvious during our intense rush to pack up and sell our house to get to Massachusetts in sixty days or less was the remembrance of leaving other homes as a part of growing up. Remembrances of physically leaving home as house, family, neighborhood, or country; remembrances of metaphorically leaving home as letting go and moving on from the emotional ties and spiritual bonds that define us.

From my past leavings, I now know that each of us must face decisions about our good-byes to places and people, jobs and careers, hopes and dreams, as well as to disappointments, hurts, rejections, and betrayals that may haunt us from the past. Indeed, sometimes we choose, unconsciously, to leave old assumptions about how life is and what God and religion and worship may be about. Other times, we leave and no one in the world knows we have left but us. And then there are those times when we ourselves may not even know we have departed. That happened to me in a previous marriage, when for years my mind and spirit resided elsewhere, in a job that had clearly not been me for a long time, and even in a pew where I sat for years without ever really being there.

By the same token I also know that because letting go can be difficult, painful, or inconvenient, we sometimes stay rather than say good-bye. We stay, holding on to old habits and hopes, longings and loves, notions and beliefs about manners and morals that are more in the marrow than the brain. We stay, circling around and ignoring the possibility that late in life fears, hopes, and certainties from childhood that still drive our adult decisions and fashion our attitudes will surprise us.

While making the choice to stay in Toledo or to leave for Northampton, Ted and I experienced tension in our relationship as well as within ourselves. To hold on or to let go became a yin-yang experience pulling our bodies, minds, and spirits in both directions. Good-bye and Hello both have a cost and a promise, we acknowledged as though for the first time. But it wasn't the first time. The thoughts, feelings, aha's, and unknowings were most familiar. After all, we experienced many variations on the theme when we each decided to be in relationship, marry, and create a home— when we each decided to say "Good-bye" to the last day of one life and "Hello" to the first day of a new one.

"In those days Jesus came from Nazareth of Galilee. . . ." Not everyone assumes that Jesus experienced this tension of deciding about staying or leaving. There are those who read Jesus' life as carefully scripted by God from before the beginning and assume that he was simply being faithful to what was foreordained. But consider the possibility that Jesus, like you and me, was faced with wide-ranging choices about "Hello" and "Good-bye" in his life, and that like us he, too, experienced tension when deciding, "Should I stay or should I leave?"

Assuming that Jesus of Nazareth is like us, wonder about him deciding not to leave Nazareth but to stay there. Countless Sunday school stories and sermons have told us that he did not leave until he was an adult—perhaps thirty years old. Hence, it is reasonable to suppose that Jesus contemplated leaving Nazareth earlier and more than once but chose instead to stay.

The point of such an exploration is not to grade Jesus and judge whether he made the right or wrong choice. It is not about evaluating his timing or about whether he should have done it sooner or later. It is not even about our doing it the way Jesus did. What the Jesus questions can do is spotlight some of the Nazareths in my life and yours—here and now. Speculating on Jesus' choice-making process may well reflect the importance of our own Nazareths and thus awaken some new awareness of the ways you and I define who and what we are and who and what we will become.

Moreover, once we can name some of our Nazareths—especially the one that contains and holds us either secure and comfortable or trapped and bound—we begin taking our first step toward finding Jesus as a way to discover ourselves. A friend wrote a journal article entitled "It's Nice to Know What You're Doing." It is more than nice. It can be life saving and life giving to name our Nazareth and ask, "Is this nurturing or killing me?"

To stay or to leave? To hold on or to let go? To say "Good-bye" or "Hello"? In the midst of all those carefully labeled boxes, Ted and I knew it was not simply about geography or moving vans. Henry David Thoreau said that he "traveled extensively in Concord." Journeys that have been awaiting us for a long time often start and end in the same town or under the same roof, around a familiar dining room table, or standing before our bathroom mirror. The choice to stay or leave begins by risking consciousness of what our Nazareth is and whether or not to name it a city of Life.

Wanderings and Wonderings

"In those days Jesus came from Nazareth. . . ."
If Jesus *came from Nazareth*, it means he left home.

- Why might he have chosen to leave?
- Who and what did he leave behind?
- What could he gain by acting on that decision?
- What might he lose?
- What is the cost of his *not* leaving?
- And the promise of his leaving?

- Do you believe Jesus just picked up one day and left Nazareth, or do you believe he may have thought about leaving or actually attempted to leave at other times and then decided to stay instead?

Nazareth for Jesus was a geographical place, but Nazareth can also be a symbolic way of thinking about jobs, relationships, institutions, convictions, addictions, securities, obsessions, fears, and hopes.

Name your Nazareth—perhaps one of several.

- List the promises, benefits, and gains of staying there.
- List the costs, downsides, and losses of staying.
- And what about the alternatives—the costs, losses, and downsides of leaving as well as the benefits, gains, and promises?

Put a symbol of your Nazareth on the floor. It could be a drawing, a legal contract, a household or office item, a piece of jewelry, a rock, a rope, or anything that says "Nazareth" to you.

Straddle this representation of your Nazareth and close your eyes. Imagine yourself leaving it, and when ready, take some steps forward. Note how you feel.

Now once more straddle your Nazareth, and with your eyes closed imagine staying. Do not move. Stay as long as you want. Again, note how you feel.

Stand astride your Nazareth one more time. With your eyes closed, imagine you are a scale holding the option of staying in one hand and the option of leaving in the other.

- Which hand feels heavier?
- What might that weight tell you about your Nazareth?
- And concerning your Nazareth, what more might you now know about your choices and your process for deciding what to do?

Mirrors

For all that has been—Thanks!
To all that shall be—Yes!
　　　　—Dag Hammarskjöld, *Markings*[6]

The truth is that our finest moments are most likely to occur when we are feeling deeply uncomfortable, unhappy, or unfulfilled. For it is only in such moments, propelled by our discomfort, that we are likely to step out of our ruts and start searching for different ways or truer answers.
　　　　—M. Scott Peck, *Abounding Grace: An Anthology of Wisdom*[7]

When a dream takes hold of you, what can you do? You can run with it, let it run your life, or let it go and think for the rest of your life about what might have been.

—Patch Adams, in the film *Patch Adams*[8]

There comes a time in life when there is nothing else to do but go your own way. . . . He had to take the big leap into the unknown far away from the safety of his reef. In order to find the real purpose in his life, Daniel Dolphin had to set aside everything that limited him.

—Sergio Bambaren, *The Dolphin: The Story of A Dreamer*[9]

Variation on a Theme by Rilke
by Denise Levertov[10]

> A certain day became a presence to me;
> there it was, confronting me—a sky, air, light:
> a being. And before it started to descend
> from the height of noon, it leaned over
> and struck my shoulder as if with
> the flat of a sword, granting me
> honor and a task. The day's blow
> rang out, metallic—or it was I, a bell awakened,
> and what I heard was my whole self
> saying and singing what it knew: I can.

From *Girl with a Pearl Earring*
by Tracy Chevalier[11]

When her eyes fell on the palette knife a shiver ran through me. I took a step forward at the same time as she moved to the cupboard and grabbed the knife. I stopped, unsure of what she would do next.

He knew though. He knew his own wife. He moved with Catharina as she stepped up to the painting. She was quick but he was quicker—he caught her by the wrist as she plunged the diamond blade of the knife towards the painting. . . . Catharina struggled but he held her wrist firmly, waiting for her to drop the knife. Suddenly she groaned. Flinging the knife away, she clutched her belly. The knife skidded across the tiles to my feet then spun and spun, slower and slower, as we all stared at it. It came to a stop with the blade pointed at me.

I was meant to pick it up. That was what maids were meant to do—pick up their master's and mistress's things and put them back in their place.

I looked up and met his eye, holding his grey gaze for a long moment. I knew it was for the last time. I did not look at anyone else. . . .

I did not pick up the knife. I turned and walked from the room, down the stairs and through the doorway. . . . I got to the street and I began to run. I ran down the Oude Langedkijck and across the bridge into Market Square.

Only thieves and children run.

I reached the center of the square and stopped in the circle of tiles with the eight-pointed star in the middle. Each indicated a direction I could take.

I could go back to my parents.

I could find Pieter at the Meat Hall and agree to marry him.

I could go to van Ruijven's house—he would take me in with a smile.

I could go to van Leeuwenhoek and ask him to take pity on me.

I could go to Rotterdam and search for Frans.

I could go back to Papists' Corner.

I could go into the New Church and pray to God for guidance.

When I made my choice, the choice I knew I had to make, I set my feet carefully along the edge of the point and went the way it told me walking steadily.

The Journey
by Mary Oliver[12]

> One day you finally knew
> what you had to do, and began,
> though the voices around you
> kept shouting
> their bad advice—
> though the whole house
> began to tremble
> and you felt the old tug
> at your ankles.
> "Mend my life!"
> each voice cried.
> But you didn't stop.
> You knew what you had to do,
> though the wind pried
> with its stiff fingers
> at the very foundations—

though their melancholy
was terrible.
It was already late
enough, and a wild night,
and the road full of fallen
branches and stones.
But little by little,
as you left their voices behind,
the stars began to burn
through the sheets of clouds,
and there was a new voice,
which you slowly
recognized as your own,
that kept you company
as you strode deeper and deeper
into the world,
determined to do
the only thing you could do—
determined to save
the only life you could save.

TWO

BEGINNING
THE JOURNEY

In those days Jesus came from Nazareth of Galilee and was baptized by John in the Jordan. And just as he was coming up out of the water, he saw the heavens torn apart and the Spirit descending like a dove on him. And a voice came from heaven, "You are my Son, the Beloved; with you I am well pleased." (Mark 1:9–11, emphasis added)

Reflections
BY CAREN

As always, my heart began to pound when the phone rang at 10:37 on a frosty December night, just a fortnight into Advent, just a week beyond lighting Hanukah candles, just days before the winter solstice. Years of living with a clergyman had taught me that an unexpected late-night call rarely bore good tidings.

As I watched Ted absorb the news, drop his jaw, ask, "What happened?" and say, "Oh no," hang up in silence, and gather his thoughts, I held my breath. "A large bale of hay rolled on Harry's partner, Jimmie," he finally reported. "Jimmie is dead."

Forty minutes up the road, the police, emergency medical responders, and Harry stood waiting for us next to the dark red barn and white clapboard farmhouse that the partners had purchased a mere month earlier. Earlier enough for them to enjoy a first Thanksgiving on their Promised Land; earlier enough to resettle the three hundred Icelandic sheep that Jimmie shepherded 24/7 no matter what the weather in the outer world or in his inner one.

Back inside the house, Harry sat amid boxes and baggage still to be unpacked. "I know that I'll feel very small again in a few days," Harry said, nodding his head. "But right now all I can do is praise God. I feel so thankful for all of God's love and grace. It's big. It's *very* big and fills me."

Big? Love? Grace? What grace? What "grace" could one find in a place where the police wouldn't even allow Harry to kneel beside his forty-three-year-old companion because the district attorney had yet to "check it out"? And because the DA hadn't arrived, Jimmie, the retired ballet dancer, who was once limber, graceful, and able to leap above audiences and over hill and dale, now had to just be—alone and frozen at a distance—as Ted recited last rites in a deep, solemn voice. As the sheep in the barn bleated and as the dogs watching over them barked. And as a disinterested policeman held a lantern projecting a long beam onto hands enveloping a worn, rain-stained prayer book, and then continued on— onto, over, and past Jimmie and into the blackness beyond.

Because of health-related issues, Harry, a playwright and former New York ad executive, could neither tend the sheep nor drive a car. Dependent on Jimmie to drive him forty miles to supermarkets, to Ted's church, to other people, to the world at large, it seemed likely that Harry would be unable to keep the farm. So what was this quality Harry so poignantly and generously named "Grace"? And why couldn't I see her as he did in the midst of such an inexplicable tragedy?

"All Jimmie felt called to be at this point in his life was a shepherd. And he got to do that before he died. He got to do that and live on this farm for one wonderful month, and Jimmie felt blessed," Harry said. "He *was* blessed. He was blessed by God's grace."

Whenever I hear the hymn "Amazing Grace," I get goose bumps. I know I'm not alone when I wonder why it gets under my skin. But I assume it's because the words speak universal truths about my yearnings and yours. Truths that can lead us to real rivers flowing with healing waters as well as metaphorical ones. Rivers that flow in religious institutions, spiritual communities, or medical and recovery centers—places that invite us to seek a Higher Power for the sake of healing and wholeness. Rivers that flow through our towns and cities or through forests and even deserts and help to sustain us and cleanse our real and imagined wounds and transgressions. And rivers that take the form of the gushes of excitement we feel coursing through every fiber of our being when we stop and listen to still, small voices that call us to leave our Nazareths to become diligent shepherds of our wildest and deepest desires.

On the night Jimmie died, the police remained distant and singularly focused on their mission. So when the DA finally arrived, declared the tragedy an accident, and decreed that the officers could carry the lifeless body up the hill, those who had come to hold Harry huddled together to witness the event. Spontaneously, as Jimmie passed between and among them, they began softly singing, "Amazing grace, how sweet the sound . . ." As the familiar tune moved through the first stanza, one friend thought she heard a young, restless policeman snickering behind her. Annoyed, she turned to rebuke him. But instead of finding the smirk she had assumed, she discovered only his tears and in them a mysterious, intangible quality that Harry called "grace." In his sermon "You Are Accepted," theologian Paul Tillich said, "Grace strikes us when we are in great pain and restlessness. . . . It strikes us when our disgust for our own being, our weakness, our hospitality, and our lack of direction and composure have become intolerable to us. It strikes us when, year after year, the longed-for perfection of life does not appear, when the old compulsions reign with us as they have for decades. . . . Sometimes at that moment a wave of light breaks into our darkness, and it is as though a voice were saying: 'You are accepted. . . .'"[13]

Three days after Jimmie died, those who cared about and loved him—family members, clergy, dancers, musicians, shepherds, and other friends—arrived at True North Farm. Six men and women awkwardly carried his hand-built coffin down the hill and placed it on a riverbank. Sheep baaed in the background, and a blues harmonica wailed above the mourners. Together we prayed, sang, and reflected. And by the end, after sprinkling river water on the simple pine box, we knew that the spirit of God's love, forgiveness, and grace had, indeed, joined us to baptize, bless, and say farewell to a partner, brother, friend, uncle, and fellow shepherd.

Wanderings and Wonderings

We don't know why Jesus chooses to be baptized by John. The gospel writers never raised that question. All we know is that Jesus leaves Nazareth and goes to a river where John preaches an apocalyptic message calling people to a baptism of repentance for the forgiveness of sins. And once there, and for reasons still unexplained, Jesus enters the very waters that his ancestors crossed on the way to the Promised Land.

- From what or whom may Jesus be seeking liberation when he leaves Nazareth?

- What streams of thought about his life and the people in the world around him might he have followed to reach that decision?

Recall Bible stories about the Tabernacle, the portable sanctuary the early Israelites erected in the wilderness. Inside was the Holy of Holies. In turn, the Holy of Holies contained the Ark of the Covenant and the Ten Commandments, which were separated from the rest of the structure by a curtain. The Tabernacle represented the dwelling of God in the midst of the Israelites. They carried it with them after the exodus. During King Solomon's reign, the Temple replaced the Tabernacle. When the Jewish people were exiled in Babylonia during the sixth century BCE, the Tabernacle was carried away and never again found.

Name the heavens, havens, homes, or even hiding places where God is said to be residing in the world around you.

- Where do you, personally, imagine God resides?

Coming up out of the water, Jesus looks up and sees the heavens open and the Spirit descending upon him.

- What might this imply about the mysterious nature of God's dwelling place?

At the end of the narratives that describe Jesus' death, the curtain at the door of the Holy of Holies in the Jerusalem Temple tears from top to bottom. Originally, the New Testament was written in Greek, and the word describing the tearing can also be translated as "rip" or "rend." The same Greek word for "tearing" is used when the heavens open at Jesus' baptism in Mark's gospel.

- If God were to escape from the institutional walls or stained glass or liturgies or theologies of our day, what do you imagine might happen?
- What do we accomplish by keeping the Divine in that container— safely exiled from the ordinary?
- How do you "contain" and keep distant and hidden that which is called Mystery, the Other, the Divine in your life?
- Do institutions and long-standing attitudes, convictions, rules, ambivalence, and indifference play a role in your choices to do that?
- If you were to peek inside that container or even rip it wide open, what do you imagine you would let loose?
- How do you keep your Holy of Holies pure and separate from everything else in your world and your life?

Ponder what, if anything, that might say about your most intimate connections to the sacred and/or the profane.

A voice from heaven tells Jesus he is a beloved son who is well pleasing. Close your eyes. Silently or aloud say, "You are my Son, the Beloved; with you I am well pleased." Then in your mind's eye, see Jesus and imagine his unspoken response.

Now visualize what it would be like for you to have God descend upon you. Ask yourself:

- If that were to happen in my life, what might I have to give up or take on?
- The word *beloved*—what does it mean to be a beloved one?

Look around your office or school or dining room table and wonder:

- Who has ever called me a beloved son, daughter, friend, spouse, lover, or colleague?
- From whom do I yearn to hear those words?
- To whom have I given that blessing?
- Who has waited and still waits to hear me say, "You are my beloved in whom I am well pleased"?

Mirrors

We are not human beings having a spiritual experience. We are spiritual beings having a human experience.
    —Pierre Teilhard de Chardin[14]

i thank You God for this most amazing day: for the leaping greenly spirits of trees and a blue true dream of sky; and for everything which is natural which is infinite which is yes.
    —e. e. cummings, *Complete Poems 1913–1962*[15]

As rivers have their source in some far off fountain, so the human spirit has its source. To find his fountain of spirit is to learn the secret of heaven and earth.
    —Lao Tzu[16]

Baptism is a beginning, not the end.
    —Sledge, in the film *Tender Mercies*[17]

From *I and Thou*
by Martin Buber[18]

You know always in your heart that you need God more than everything: but do you not know that God needs you—in the fullness of His eternity needs you? How would man be, how would you be, if God did not need him, did not need you? You need God, in order to be—and God needs you, for the very meaning of your life. In instruction and in poems men are at pains to say more, and they say too much—what turgid and presumptuous talk that is about the "God who becomes"; but we know unshakably in our hearts that there is a becoming of the God that is. The world is not divine sport, it is divine destiny. There is divine meaning in the life of the world, of man, of human persons, of you and of me.

I Will Not Die an Unlived Life
by Dawna Markova[19]

> I will not die an unlived life,
> I will not live in fear
> of falling or catching fire.
> I choose to inhabit my days,
> to allow my living to open me,
> to make me less afraid,
> more accessible,
> to loosen my heart
> until it becomes a wing,
> a torch, a promise.
> I choose to risk my significance,
> to live so that which came to me as seed
> goes to the next as blossom,
> and that which came to me as blossom,
> goes on as fruit.

La Poesia
by Pablo Neruda[20]

> . . . And something ignited in my soul,
> fever or unremembered wings,
> and I went my own way,
> deciphering
> that burning fire

and I wrote the first bare line,
bare, without substance, pure
foolishness,
pure wisdom
of one who knows nothing,
and suddenly I saw
the heavens
unfastened
and open.

THREE

LIVING WITH WILDERNESS

Then Jesus was led up by the Spirit into the wilderness to be tempted by the devil. He fasted forty days and forty nights, and afterwards he was famished. The tempter came and said to him, "If you are the Son of God, command these stones to become loaves of bread."

But he answered, "It is written, 'One does not live by bread alone, but by every word that comes from the mouth of God.'"

Then the devil took him to the holy city and placed him on the pinnacle of the temple, saying to him, "If you are the Son of God, throw yourself down; for it is written, 'He will command his angels concerning you,' and 'On their hands they will bear you up, so that you will not dash your foot against a stone.'"

Jesus said to him, "Again it is written, 'Do not put the Lord your God to the test.'"

Again, the devil took him to a very high mountain and showed him all the kingdoms of the world and their splendor; and he said to him, "All these I will give you, if you will fall down and worship me."

Jesus said to him, "Away with you, Satan! for it is written, 'Worship the Lord your God, and serve only him.'" Then the devil left him, and suddenly angels came and waited on him. (Matthew 4:1–11)

Reflections
BY CAREN

In 1988, I fasted for three days on an uninhabited island off the coast of Maine. The solo retreat was part of a rugged eleven-day Outward Bound (OB) sailing expedition for midlife men and women seeking new horizons in their literal and psychic worlds.

Except for the solo retreat, thirteen of us lived as canned sardines do—in a container the shape of a thirty-foot sailboat with no bathroom, galley, or engine. We ranged in age from forty-one (me) to sixty-something; we ranged in fitness from passable to excellent. As for sailing experience, I helped define the spectrum. My experience was raw—zilch. Fortunately, among the seven women and six men on board, a few sported seasoned sea legs.

Most of us signed up for OB hypothesizing that the most difficult challenge would be mental, not physical. However, just hours after introductions and basic training, we knew our theory wouldn't hold much water. First, we had to swim a hundred yards in forty-five-degree water to prove we could. Soon thereafter, we boarded the boat, tucked our gear and bodies into less than three square feet of personal living space apiece, and realized the long oars roped together down the center of the boat would do double-duty as our communal mattress. And then, after finally setting sail, there was that delicate subject someone brought up. "There's no bathroom," that someone said. "You're right," replied an instructor, who proceeded to sit on the edge of the boat and discreetly lower her butt below the frame while sliding her shorts to her ankles. "Got it? It's not rocket science."

To analyze every reason why I signed up for such a foreign expedition to help me discern how I was to be or not to be on the next leg of my journey to adulthood is fruitless. In retrospect, all I know is that I felt both led and driven to head there. Perhaps there were hints of such a journey during my rebellious childhood. Perhaps when I eloped with a man of another faith and my father mourned. Perhaps later, when my husband and I explained our decision to divorce to our children. That night, as we told my daughter, Jamie, nine, and son, Evan, six, that two no longer added up to one, I watched my relationship with Jamie shatter. And in the years that followed, my efforts to piece it back together failed.

The first time I heard about Outward Bound, I convinced myself it might be the glue gun I needed to bind the shards we kept in separate rooms. So on her fourteenth birthday, I gifted her with an OB catalog and an offer to sign up for any program. I renewed the unaccepted offer during the winter holidays and on birthdays after that. Each time she refused. That is, until days after turning sixteen, when she made a daring statement about what *outward bound*, not Outward Bound, meant. In an act of self-renunciation, she ran away from home.

In a desperate search for clues of Jamie's whereabouts, I found crumpled OB catalogs under her bed, at the back of her closet, and on top of a pile marked "TRASH!!!!!" At seventeen, when Jamie returned and chose to live with her father, I failed to resist the temptation to try again. This time I watched as she held it high over the trash, turned her face from mine, and with a disgusted look dropped it.

While beating myself up for being a stupid, thickheaded, insensitive, unconscious, impotent parent, I shook remnants of the previous night's dinner off the soaked pages and began thumbing through them. Convinced I knew every course listed, I did a double take upon seeing one for adults forty-plus. "Where did it come from? Has it always been there? Why does it intrigue me? Sailing? I don't know a damn thing about it. Hiking? Never been on a serious one. Rock climbing, rappelling, and a ropes course? You gotta be kidding. A three-day solo in the wilderness . . ."

Checking older catalogs, I discovered the sailing course always landed on the same page. Looking at the picture of the boat, the ocean, and a place in Maine hundreds of miles from any world I had ever known, I heard Rabbi Hillel the Elder's ancient voice: "If I am not for myself, then who will be for me? And if I am only for myself, then what am I? If not now, when?"

When? Then—when after my divorce I worked two jobs for sixty hours weekly to support us. Then—when I left a good newspaper job without another to pick up the slack. Then—when I exiled myself to a psychic wasteland littered with self-pity, blame, rationalizations, justifications, and explanations. Now—that place in my life where an irretrievable past continued to have power over me. Now—when my decade-long relationship to another man had to end. Now—when I wanted so much to be the parent I never had and had never been. Now—when I looked with new eyes at painful questions and felt I didn't need to fix something, have an answer, be more than I was, be more than I was hoping I could become. Now— when for each hope of the future was a page waiting for me to fill in the blanks. Now—if not now, when?

They say that you don't pick your solo island at Outward Bound. It picks you. Mine looked impenetrable, hostile. I could only reach its borders at high tide. To go anywhere I would have needed a machete to slice through thorny thickets and cut tangled vines. Creatures I couldn't see let me know they saw me. At low tide, the cliff leading to the sea was a sea of mud. The only plus was that my personal space had expanded to a twenty-foot circle to amble around in.

Throughout three 95-degree days and two 40-degree nights, I sat, stood, walked in circles, gazed over the edge of the cliff, journaled, slept, watched my shadow grow long and grow short, and visited the only other places I could—painful corners of my past and an unscripted future. Invited or not, the living and the dead, who inhabited the crowded waiting rooms of my imagination, visited. Parents, children, siblings, relatives, teachers, rabbis, an ex-husband, employers, false idols, friends, lovers, enemies, devils, angels, and beasts invaded my tiny circle. Each told stories. Some sounded familiar; others I never heard or chose to hear before. Compelling stories that tempted me to step through safety nets and over self-imposed boundaries and explore those parts of my inner landscape that mirrored my island. Dark, messy, and frightening corners of my body, mind, and spirit where attitudes, feelings, emotions, behaviors, and desires needed to be separated like wheat and chaff if I was ever to transform a dead end into a healing path. An ancient Chinese saying came to mind: "A crisis is an opportunity sailing on the wind."

On the third day I stepped off the island and onto the sailboat, and I was very hungry. Not only for food, but to begin living my story anew. I felt indebted to the crisis that brought me to the valley of the shadow of death so I could face mine own enemies, anoint myself with healing oil, see my cup runneth over, and feel blessed with a new understanding of goodness and mercy that still follows me.

In those days—almost two decades ago—I landed on the same shore when I returned home but stood in a different place. I could see my career path, I ended my long-term relationship, and I sought forgiveness from those I had intentionally or unconsciously hurt. The list was long. One day, I found the courage to call Jamie and asked if we could talk. But we didn't. Instead, when we met, we just exchanged the curious glances and stares that strangers on a boat do from a distance until gusting winds of change violently rock everything. Feeling that the moment had come to leave yet another wilderness, I risked walking toward Jamie with open arms—silently, slowly, and with trepidation.

Wanderings and Wonderings

In the original Greek, the gospel stories were neither separated into chapters and verses nor punctuated. Consequently, in the earliest accounts of Jesus' baptism, the last sentence—"You are my Son, the Beloved; with you I am well pleased"—is followed at once by the opening sentences of his wilderness experiences.

Close your eyes and revisit images of Jesus at his baptism, going down into the water and then coming back up, encountering the dove and hearing that he is the beloved Son of God. See yourself in the wilderness that Jesus will enter. Take a long look at everything around you—near and far. Be curious and engage your imagination as you ask yourself:

- How does Jesus look?
- What thoughts, fears, concerns, certainties, doubts, other feelings, and questions might be spinning around in his head? And his heart?

In Mark's gospel, the same Spirit that just blessed Jesus in the Jordan River *immediately drives* him into the wilderness. In Matthew and Luke, the same Spirit *leads* him instead. Pause and in your mind's eye see Jesus being driven by the Spirit. Then see him being led by the Spirit.

- Does the story change when you picture Jesus being *immediately driven* into the wilderness instead of led? How?

Describe what the Spirit might want Jesus to experience, learn, discover, and know about himself *immediately* after hearing, "You are my Son, the Beloved; with you I am well pleased."

- What might the Spirit want Jesus to know about the world?
- And about God?

Re-read the passage and observe that in the opening words we learn that the tempter's agenda is to test Jesus. In Greek, the word for "test" can also mean "tempt" or "put to the test." Look up or recall other words for "test."

- In today's world, what things, ideas, and situations test us?

Write in your journal about a time when you felt as though your life depended upon a particular test, and recall the feelings you experienced during and afterwards.

In Jesus' time, Roman forces controlled Jerusalem. Historical accounts report that poverty contributed to political, military, and religious unrest that went beyond the walls of the city and into the countryside. Roman officials, Temple tithes and taxes, and the expansion of large estates that swallowed up small family farms imposed extraordinary financial burdens and frightening prospects for the future upon the Jews. Landowners, merchants, fishermen, and others who had been self-sufficient faced the reality that they would forfeit their farms, businesses, and other enterprises upon failing to pay taxes. They would then become day laborers and unemployed, homeless "expendables."

According to the text, the tempter tests Jesus three times. Each time Jesus rejects the offer and states, "It is written." He then quotes passages from Hebrew Scripture attributed to Moses. The first time the tempter challenges Jesus to turn stones into bread. Imagine what people in Jesus' time would be saying to each other about him if he could change stones to bread.

- What, for him, would be the positive side of accepting the tempter's offer and being able to do that?
- And the downside?

The second time the tempter takes Jesus to the pinnacle of the Temple in Jerusalem. The tempter then challenges Jesus to throw himself down and quotes Psalm 91:11–12: "For it is written, 'He will command his angels concerning you,' and 'On their hands they will bear you up, so that you will not dash your foot against a stone.'" Once again Jesus rebuffs the tempter. Go beyond the obvious reason he may have chosen not to be hooked by this test by making two lists. Again imagine what life may have been like for first-century Jewish people who were poor, sick, or just one tax payment away from losing all. On one side list the costs and promises, pros and cons, benefits and liabilities Jesus might have considered if he were to throw himself down. On the other side, write down the costs and promises of not succumbing to temptation.

Finally, the tempter shows Jesus all the kingdoms of the world and their splendor and says, "All these I will give you, if you will fall down and worship me." In your journal describe your reaction to this offer and take into consideration the other temptations. Then describe what you imagine Jesus really stood personally to gain or to lose by accepting instead of rejecting each of them.

The passage ends with Jesus dismissing the tempter with the words: "Away with you, Satan! for it is written, 'Worship the Lord your God, and serve only him.'" Note that this is the first time Jesus refers to his tempter as "Satan."

- Why, after being blessed at his baptism, might the same Spirit have driven Jesus to a wilderness to deal with these issues?
- As he leaves the wilderness, to what is Jesus saying no?
- To what might he be saying yes?
- What might he know about tests, temptations, himself, and God that he didn't know before? And still not know?

Make a list of words that describe *wilderness* for you. Then, using whatever art supplies are handy—paper, pencils, crayons, pens, paints, clay, straw, rocks, grass, leaves, sand, dirt—create an expression of *wilderness*. Placing your representation in front of you, wonder about such places in our geographical, political, and spiritual worlds today. Name wilderness places that we encounter. Looking back, recall a specific wilderness in your life.

- Were you *driven* or *led* there?
- Why do you call it a wilderness?

- What experiences with tests, temptations, and new questions, possibilities, choices, and decisions did you have while you were there?
- How were you different after spending forty days or hours or weeks or years in that place?

Where do you find yourself in a wilderness today—here and now? Is it in a relationship that matters, in your job, within your family, in terms of your health or aging, in your spiritual community, or as a stage of your spiritual journey? From within that wilderness, what are you discovering about temptations to

- Provide for others?
- Defy natural laws?
- Seek power?

As for questions in your wilderness:

- To what are you saying yes or no?
- And to which questions are you saying neither yes nor no but choosing, instead, to live with ambiguity or even considering "both/and" instead of "either/or"?
- What are you discovering there that you could learn in no other way?
  - About tests, temptations, devils, and even angels?
  - About being hungry?
  - About your world? Yourself? God?

In ancient texts, another name for Satan is Lucifer, which is translated as "light bringer."

- How might Satan "enlighten" Jesus in the wilderness?
- When you met Satan in the darkest places of one of your wildernesses, what might you have seen for the first time?
- Today, here, now, in your world and life, what, if anything, may Satan be bringing into the light?

Mirrors

If you therefore go to the desert to be rid of all the dreadful people and all the awful problems in your life, you will be wasting your time. You should go to the desert for a total confrontation with yourself. For one goes to the desert to see more and to see better. One goes to the desert especially to take a closer look at the things and people one would rather not see, to face situations one would rather avoid, to answer questions one would rather forget.

> —Alessandro Pronzato, from *The Desert: An Anthology for Lent* by John Moses[21]

To find in ourselves what makes life worth living is risky business, for it means that once we know, we must seek it. It also means that without it the life will be valueless.

> —Marsha Sinetar, *Ordinary People as Monks and Mystics: Lifestyles for Self-Discovery*[22]

There is a physical desert, inhabited by a few exceptional men and women who are called to live there; but more importantly, there is an inner desert, into which each one of us must one day venture. It is a void; an empty space for solitude and testing.

> —Frère Ivan, from *The Desert: An Anthology for Lent* by John Moses[23]

March 3, 1969. In ten days we leave here to start back to Kentucky. For half a year now we've lived a life radically unlike the life we've chosen and made there at home. What I get from the experience out here is the awareness that the life we want is not merely the one we have chosen and made; it is the one we must be choosing and making. To keep it alive we must be perpetually choosing it and making its differences from among all contrary and alternative possibilities. We must accept the pain and labor of that, or we lose its satisfactions and its joy. Only by risking it, offering it freely to its possibilities, can we keep it.

> —Wendell Berry, *A Continuous Harmony: Essays Cultural and Agricultural*[24]

From *Touching the Void*
by Joe Simpson[25]

Slowly it dawned on me that my new world, for all its warmth and beauty, was little better than the crevasse. I was 200 feet above the glacier and six miles from base camp. The tranquility evaporated, and a familiar tension returned. The crevasse had been only a starter! How foolish to have thought that I had done it, that I was safe! I stared at distant moraines and glimmers of light from the lakes, and felt crushed. It was too far, too much. I wasn't strong enough. I had no food, no water, nothing, and again I felt the menace surrounding me. I almost believed that I wasn't going to be allowed to escape; whatever I did would lead to another barrier, and then another, until I stopped and gave in. The black moraines and glittering lake water in the distance mocked any hopes of escape. I was in a malevolent place; a tangible hostility enclosed me as if the air had been charged with static electricity. This was not the playground we had walked into so long ago.

I sat up and looked bitterly at the frayed rope-end which I had carried up from the crevasse.

"This is getting ridiculous," I said aloud quietly, as if afraid something might hear me and know I was beaten.

As I gazed at the distant moraines I knew that I must at least try. I would probably die out there amid those boulders. The thought didn't alarm me. It seemed reasonable, matter-of-fact. That was how it was. I could aim for something. If I died, well, that wasn't so surprising, but I wouldn't have just waited for it to happen. The horror of dying no longer affected me as it had in the crevasse. I now had the chance to confront it and struggle against it. It wasn't a bleak dark terror anymore, just fact, like my broken leg and frostbitten fingers, and I couldn't be afraid of things like that. My leg would hurt when I fell, and when I couldn't get up I would die. In a peculiar way it was refreshing to be faced with simple choices. It made me feel sharp and alert, and I looked ahead at the land stretching into distant haze and saw my part in it with a greater clarity and honesty than I had ever experienced before.

Insomnia
by Dana Gioia[26]

Now you hear what the house has to say.
Pipes clanking, water running in the dark,
the mortgaged walls shifting in discomfort,
and voices mounting in an endless drone
of small complaints like the sounds of a family
that year by year you've learned how to ignore.

But now you must listen to the things you own,
all that you've worked for these past years,
the murmur of property, of things in disrepair,
the moving parts about to come undone,
and twisting in the sheets remember all
the faces you could not bring yourself to love.

How many voices have escaped you until now,
the venting furnace, the floorboards underfoot,
the steady accusations of the clock
numbering the minutes no one will mark.
The terrible clarity this moment brings,
the useless insight, the unbroken dark.

From *Book of Hours: Love Poems to God*
by Ranier Maria Rilke[27]

We must not portray you in king's robes,
you drifting mist that brought forth the morning.

Once again from the old paintboxes
we take the same gold for scepter and crown
that has disguised you through the ages.

Piously we produce our images of you
till they stand around you like a thousand walls.
And when our hearts would simply open,
our fervent hands hide you.

FOUR

RETURNING HOME

Then Jesus, filled with the power of the Spirit, returned to Galilee, and a report about him spread through all the surrounding country. He began to teach in their synagogues and was praised by everyone. When he came to Nazareth, where he had been brought up, he went to the synagogue on the sabbath day, as was his custom. He stood up to read, and the scroll of the prophet Isaiah was given to him. He unrolled the scroll and found the place where it was written:

> The Spirit of the Lord is upon
>   me,
> because he has anointed me
>   to bring good news to the poor.
> He has sent me to proclaim release
>   to the captives
> and recovery of sight to the
>   blind,
>   to let the oppressed go free,
> to proclaim the year of the Lord's
>   favor.

And he rolled up the scroll, gave it back to the attendant, and sat down. The eyes of all in the synagogue were fixed on him. Then he began to say to them, "Today this scripture has been fulfilled in your hearing." All spoke well of him and were amazed at the gracious words that came from his mouth. They said, "Is not this Joseph's son?"

He said to them, "Doubtless you will quote to me this proverb, 'Doctor, cure yourself!' And you will say, 'Do here also in your hometown the things that we have heard you did at Capernaum.'" And he said, "Truly I tell you, no prophet is accepted in the prophet's hometown. But the truth is, there were many widows in Israel in the time of Elijah, when the heaven was shut up three years and six months, and there was a severe famine over all the land; yet Elijah was sent to none of them except to a widow at Zarephath in Sidon. There were also many lepers in Israel in the time of the prophet Elisha, and none of them was cleansed except Naaman the Syrian." When they heard this, all in the synagogue were filled with rage. They got up, drove him out of the town, and led him to the brow of the hill on which their town was built, so that they might hurl him off the cliff. But he passed through the midst of them and went on his way. (Luke 4:14–30)

Reflections
BY BILL

I was home from college for the weekend. As I walked onto the front porch of the house I had grown up in, in Govans, a suburb of Baltimore, I was surprised and mystified by a sign in the front widow reading "This House Is Not for Sale." Why, I wondered, was it there? I could understand "For Sale," but why in the world "Not for Sale"?

Unsettled by my question, my father explained with emotion that our Radnor Avenue middle-class neighborhood, with row houses and a few old single houses like ours, was the target of "block busters." In the mid-1950s, these real estate speculators singled out areas in which they would buy one house on a "white" street and then move in a black family. With a panic of "changing neighborhood" in the air, real estate prices plummeted as white flight to the suburbs got under way. Seizing the opportunity to acquire properties at rock-bottom prices, realtors bought the vacant homes, inflated the prices, and resold them to black families waiting to move in. My father was one of a small group of white homeowners who could not afford moving out and who banded together futilely to hold the color line.

I was indignant and offended that my parents would participate in what I considered discrimination and prejudice. From my white male perch, safe and secure in a university in the Blue Ridge Mountains of Virginia, my father was no more than a redneck bigot. Not until years later, when I returned home to his house on a different street, did I realize that 507 Radnor Avenue was the only investment for the future my father had. And before his eyes, he was watching it disappear. His eldest son, blinded by virtue and self-righteousness, playing the role of holier-than-thou social critic, could not appreciate his father's predicament. As was his style when hurt or misunderstood, my father simply became silent and turned away. I had been insensitive, arrogant, and judgmental even though I'd been speaking the truth.

Going home can be costly. Having been in a different place, we think home looks different when we return. Home can be an old house or a wounded parent or a marriage of thirty years or even one's own self. Home is wherever we start from. And growing up means leaving and then returning there to know it for the first time. Going home is never easy. It is about arriving again—as if for the first time—and recognizing the fault lines, hurts, and heartbreaks. By never leaving, or by departing and never going back, we circle around and avoid the long healing journey to the heart of who we are and what we are about.

Returning home promises what the poet David Whyte describes as "opening of eyes long closed. . . . It is the heart after years of secret conversing speaking out loud in the clear air."[28] As long as you live only what is remembered and expected, and refrain from saying what you see and even feel when you return, it will go smoothly. You will be welcomed and praised. But should you speak a truth that reaches across lines and over boundaries, challenging the conventional wisdom of parents or golf partners or others in the pew, you are asking for trouble. Sticking with the script and doing what is customary will amaze those who cannot believe how big you have gotten and how well you read. But rage is what you stir up when you meddle where you don't belong anymore.

> The Spirit of the Lord is upon me, because he has anointed me to bring good news to the poor. He has sent me to proclaim release to the captives and recovery of sight to the blind, to let the oppressed go free, to proclaim the year of the Lord's favor.

In ancient times, prophets, priests, and kings were anointed, which endowed them not with divinity but with responsibility, and clothed them with the authority to be heard and to make important things happen. Anointing often turned prophets into meddlers. They came to see with new eyes, recognizing that being poor is about more than not having money, that not all captives are behind prison bars. They understood that freedom and oppression are not just about the petty politics of the day, but also about the politics of the heart and school classroom and office and family. And understanding, they were compelled to meddle.

Anointed or not, the life and teachings of Jesus reflect Moses' vision of "the year of the Lord's favor," a Jubliee Sabbath of Sabbaths, when every fifty years wealth and land would be redistributed, slaves set free, and debts wiped out in a version of a world starting over again. Meddlers then and now—see visions of new possibilities when they look around the world. They risk reputation and even life speaking of what they see.

This is what Jesus did. And when Jesus—or anyone like him—goes home and calls for healing, he will most likely get into trouble: Not in our backyard! We work hard to hide our poverty, act like liberated people, pretend we see everything, live the illusion of being free, and preach a lot about how God loves everyone. But don't press it. We got along fine without you when you left, and we'll do quite well when you head out of town again. Send us a postcard sometime.

Wonderings and Wanderings

Luke tells us that on leaving the wilderness and being tested, Jesus is filled with the power of the Spirit. Consider his options about what to do next, and then wonder why he returns to Galilee and goes to synagogue "as was his custom." What might Luke be telling you about Jesus the Jew as he goes home?

Jesus reads from a scroll containing text written about 520 BCE, when Jews, exiled and held captive in Babylon for seventy years, began returning home to Jerusalem. In the scroll the prophet Isaiah envisions the future. Luke seems to suggest that Isaiah's words offer a clue to how Jesus' life will be committed to a radical reordering of human community. Is it possible that Luke wants us to see people in Jesus' homeland enduring a form of captivity and oppression that echoes their Jewish ancestors' ordeal in Babylon centuries earlier? Think about the ways the Romans and temple priests might be keeping these people poor and blind to what is happening to them. Under such conditions, what would a Jubilee Year in Galilee in the first century look like?

Imagine the gracious words and comments Jesus' neighbors make to one another as they describe how he has changed since they saw him last.

- Why is a prophet not commonly accepted in his hometown?
- What might Jesus have said or done in the synagogue that could incite so much anxiety and anger that they want to throw him off the cliff?

In your Nazareth hometown—or wherever your Galilee may be—who are among the poor, blind, captive, and oppressed?

- What might be good news to those in poverty there?
- Should the blind recover their sight, what might they begin to see?

- How would the world change if those who are oppressed in your Galilee were to be set free?
- Starting creation over again with a Jubilee Year would be welcomed by whom? Resisted by whom?

Reckon the cost and promise to you and those who matter to you most upon hearing good news, being released from binds, seeing for a change, being free, proclaiming that it is a new ball game, another chapter, a chance to start all over again.

- Ask yourself about a truth in your head and heart waiting to be spoken and heard for the sake of healing a world, nation, church, family, or even yourself.
- How might the choices before you determine whether your friends and colleagues say gracious words about you or, enraged, attempt to throw you off a cliff?
- How might the edge of a cliff outside of town be the place that your healing begins?

Mirrors

We shall not cease from exploration
And the end of all our exploring
Will be to arrive where we started
And know the place for the first time.
  —T. S. Eliot, *The Complete Poems and Plays*[29]

Life can only be understood backwards, but must be lived forwards.
      —Sören Kierkegaard, from *Sunbeams: A Book of Quotations*
        by Sy Syfransky[30]

Education is all about departures,
when things are right
nobody comes home the same.
      —Stephen Dunn, *New and Selected Poems 1974–1994*[31]

To return to the source of things one has to travel in the opposite direction.
      —René Daumal, from *René Daumal: The Life and Work*
        of a Mystic Guide by Kathleen Rosenblatt[32]

Blue in Green (for Chris)
by Denver Butson[33]

our anguish is of course
the light through the glass
on the window sill

everything that walks in the sun
is a door that could lead us somewhere else
if we let it

sometimes our houses stand
and sometimes they fall

the direction of the wind has very little to do with it

sometimes we surrender
and sometimes we put our hands
in our pockets
and keep on not fighting

I Go Back to the House for a Book
by Billy Collins[34]

I turn around on the gravel
and go back to the house for a book,
something to read at the doctor's office,
and while I am inside, running the finger
of inquisition along a shelf,

another me that did not bother
to go back to the house for a book
heads out on his own,
rolls down the driveway,
and swings left toward town,

a ghost in his ghost car,
another knot in the string of time,
a good three minutes ahead of me—
a spacing that will now continue
for the rest of my life.

Sometimes I think I see him
a few people in front of me on a line
or getting up from a table

to leave the restaurant just before I do,
slipping into his coat on the way out the door.

But there is no catching him,
no way to slow him down
and put us back in sync,
unless one day he decides to go back
to the house for something,

but I cannot imagine
for the life of me what that might be.
He is out there always before me,
blazing my trail, invisible scout,
hound that pulls me along,

shade I am doomed to follow,
my perfect double,
only bumped an inch into the future,
and not nearly as well-versed as I
in the love poems of Ovid—

I who went back to the house
that fateful winter morning and got the book.

Words Never Worked (From *Your Mythic Journey*)
Jean (last name withheld)[35]

The eight of us—plus poor old Elizabeth McCarthy before she dropped
dead in the attic room—lived in a huge beat-up asbestos house in small-
town Massachusetts. The place was a wreck. . . .

Our gangly household was centered around one basic taboo: no real
conversation allowed. In a thousand unspoken ways we were discouraged
from saying anything substantial to one another. Father waited up every
night for Mother to come home . . . and as soon as she was in the door
they started up their noisy battles. Over and over they shouted the same
accusations, but since neither one ever listened you couldn't really call it
communication. . . .

Two years ago Mother insisted, as she always does, that everyone come
home for Thanksgiving dinner. I knew it was impossible, for the hundredth
time the desire to be at ease, to be part of a family that *talked* to one
another got the best of me. We assembled, thirteen of us now, dead-ended
around the living room, wondering what to say to one another, fighting the

urge to switch on the television. Mother was in the kitchen completing the last details of peas, onions, mashed potatoes, sweet potatoes, pickles, jellies, bread, pies, strong Irish coffee—and placed it, chilled and steaming, on the long table while the rest of us watched.

After she lifted her fork Mother excused herself, went upstairs, overdosed herself with barbiturates, and passed out. I found her draped on the bed and called an ambulance. At the hospital they pumped her stomach and tucked her in to sleep it off. Mother hadn't intended to die. She told me later she saw Father kissing a neighbor over the back fence and "just had to do something to change the rules." Words had never worked with them, so she gathered her most vulnerable audience and staged a statement of her anger, one which we all understood.

After the hospital phoned to say that Mother would be all right, the rest of us crept to the table and picked away at the cold feast in silence.

FIVE

WEATHERING STORMS

On that day, when evening had come, he said to them, "Let us go across to the other side." And leaving the crowd behind, they took him with them in the boat, just as he was. Other boats were with him.

A great windstorm arose, and the waves beat into the boat, so that the boat was already being swamped. But he was in the stern, asleep on the cushion; and they woke him up and said to him, "Teacher, do you not care that we are perishing?"

He woke up and rebuked the wind, and said to the sea, "Peace! Be still!" Then the wind ceased, and there was a dead calm. He said to them, "Why are you afraid? Have you still no faith?" And they were filled with great awe and said to one another, "Who then is this, that even the wind and the sea obey him?" (Mark 4:35–41)

Reflections
BY BILL

By Friday I know that I cannot bear the weekend waiting for the biopsy report from my surgery a few days earlier. When I phone I learn the doctor has been called home to Chicago where his father is very ill. He will phone me Monday when he returns. The nurse says she has the results on the desk before her and can read them to me if I want to hear them. But she quickly adds, "That is all I can do, because you must speak to the doctor about what the results mean. Do you want them?" By the tone of her voice, I know I don't. I want most to hang up and pretend it never happened and that my world is not about to tilt. Everything inside me says no as I take a deep breath and say yes. Three of the biopsy samples are clear. The fourth is malignant. The nurse does not use the word "cancer." I don't say "cancer" either. I thank her for her help and hang up.

Between Friday afternoon and Tuesday morning in the doctor's office, I live in a wilderness where my thoughts about cancer unhinge doors tightly shut and pry open windows on life and death once firmly sealed. Waiting to find out becomes an eternity of anxiety, fear, and finally, resignation. I think about things I have carefully avoided for years and fears I have managed to deny by working and exercising, living and playing hard. During those long hours between Friday and Tuesday, people around me look different, and the face in the mirror stares back more sober and real. It is a long wait.

Hearing the diagnosis without a prognosis, I do my own. I am one of those people for whom every toothache means a root canal and any ailment is terminal. Walking away from the phone feels like stepping off firm land into deep water that will become a raging storm in the hours to follow. Stormy weather is what swallows us up when the report is cancer or the lover says it is over or the slip is pink or the report card proclaims failure or Wall Street plummets and retirement hopes tremble. When waves beat on the side of the boat and we are being swamped by waters of depression, loss, endings, old wounds, new disappointments, broken promises, and shattered dreams, we get scared. With no sense that we can ever get through this on our own, we cry out. Sometimes it means praying for real for the first time, coming clean at last to an angry spouse, confessing to a rabbi or priest, no longer pretending for the therapist, admitting to ourselves, "I am afraid."

All I remember about that Tuesday morning is the doctor saying that the cancer is treatable and that given careful attention and regular exams, I will most certainly die of something else. But my most vivid recollection of all is leaving his office and, as the glass door opens into the parking garage and I head toward the car parked in a space I could still take you to today in a heartbeat, knowing that I am on the way back and will live forever. Suddenly the storm ends, the seas quiet, the wind abates. My fear is behind me and I am safe.

On the way home I recall the words of John McMurray, a doctor who died a few years earlier, describing how the most difficult moments during his cancer treatment and on his journey toward death were when he went briefly into remissions. It was during those fleeting days that he lost touch with everything that was becoming clear to him in the eye of the storm. A renewed hope of briefly avoiding death, he wrote, was the enemy of everything he was learning about life. It wasn't, I think, that he wanted to die, but rather that the storm that was upon him was the occasion for discovering a depth in relationship and meaning in the world that had eluded him until then.

I spent the week of September 11, 2001, in a motel room at San Francisco Airport waiting for a flight home. Though I could see the lights of the airport and might easily have walked there, no one was allowed near it. Airline telephone numbers were always busy. Websites were useless. On the third night I awoke at 3:00 a.m. agitated and terribly afraid. As I lay in the dark, I suddenly realized that this was the time to phone the airline! No busy signal and an operator at once. I explained where I was and asked for help to get home. She described several options. None sounded very promising. Then she said there was the chance of a Friday midday flight to Dulles. "Do you think I can be reasonably sure this will work?" I asked her. There was a long pause. She said to me, "Sir, there is only one thing of which I am certain, and that is that we are all going to die."

When I tell a friend the next morning about the conversation, he says that the operator at the airline is right. To the degree to which I can understand and live the truth of what she told me at 3:00 a.m., my anxieties and fear might become manageable. In the middle of an awful storm threatening to drown me was an opportunity to discover something new about life and its storms.

Storms are part of every life. And all our boats are small. What Jesus reminds the disciples, and even us, is that waters threatening to drown us are yet another place to tap the kind of faith that rescues, delivers, saves, even heals. There is nothing wrong or sinful about crying out and counting on parent or spouse or minister or rabbi or guru, reaching for pills or booze, going shopping or on vacation or even to bed to still the storm and quiet our fears. It is only that our habitual ways of getting through or around or over the storms rob us of learning what only storms can teach us: embracing the fear and braving the waves are the way to grow up and the opportunity to touch a spirit that filled Jesus and waits to come alive in us.

Wanderings and Wonderings

The disciples are taking Jesus across to the other side. It is evening, and there are other boats with them. Smell the sea. Imagine you are one of the disciples on the boat with Jesus as you set out and leave the crowd far behind.

Suddenly the wind picks up. The sky darkens. The waters become angry. Waves begin to beat the boat, and water washes over it, threatening to swamp everyone aboard. Describe what is happening around you and the thoughts racing wildly through your brain. Name the feelings that grip you.

Jesus is asleep on the cushion in the stern. Believing you are perishing, you awaken him. He rebukes the wind and tells it to be still; the wind ceases, and a dead calm follows. Write down what you say to yourself.

Jesus turns and asks you: "Why are you afraid? Have you still no faith?"

- Why are you afraid?
- After you wake Jesus up during the storm, what might he be implying about your assumption that he alone can save you from perishing?
- If you had had "faith," how might the outcome have been different?

Listen to your answers. Instead of responding to Jesus about your fear and lack of "faith," what do you find yourself talking about? In your journal or voice recorder, record the conversation.

Name a great storm arising on the horizon of your world, nation, community, religious community, neighborhood school, or local zoning commission.

- In what ways are those boats getting battered and being swamped?
- As the storm rises, what can you say about the fears within you?
- As you look to be saved, who is it you admire, praise, and pin hopes on to still the storm? To whom do you cry out? Or whom do you passively count on to deliver you from this storm?
- What is the missing "faith" that might make things different?
- What keeps you from looking inwardly at your fears and relying on a faith within you that could make a difference in the storm?

Look around and out to the horizon where a new storm may be approaching and threatening your own small boat—be it your marriage or career or retirement, or your anxieties during the day and dreams in the night. As waves batter and water swamps, consider the following:

- In this personal and perhaps private storm, of what are you afraid?
- Whom do you count on to rescue you and get you safely to shore?
- Are you aware of a "faith" that you have that could still the storm and see you through?
- Why do you suppose you choose to stand in awe of others who might save you?
- What prevents you from rebuking the wind yourself?

A man once said to me, I don't mind you telling me my faults, they're stale, but don't tell me my virtues. When you tell me what I could be, it terrifies me.

—Florida Scott-Maxwell, *The Measure of My Days*[36]

Our deepest fear is not that we are inadequate. Our deepest fear is that we are powerful beyond measure. It is our light, not our darkness, that most frightens us.

—Marianne Williamson, *A Return to Love: Reflections on the Principles of "A Course in Miracles"*[37]

Penetrating so many secrets,
we cease to believe in the unknowable.
But there it sits nevertheless,
calmly licking its chops.

—H. L. Mencken, from *Leadership and the New Science* by Margaret Wheatly[38]

What I thought was a brick wall turned out to be a tunnel. What I thought was an injustice turned out to be a color of the sky.

—Tony Hoagland, "A Color of the Sky," in *What Narcissism Means to Me*[39]

Come to the Edge
by Christopher Logue[40]

Come to the edge.
We might fall.
Come to the edge.
It's too high!
Come to the edge!

And they came.
And he pushed.
And they flew.

Listen to the Mustn'ts
by Shel Silverstein[41]

> Listen to the MUSTN'TS, child,
> Listen to the DON'TS
> Listen to the SHOULDN'TS
> The IMPOSSIBLES, the WON'TS
> Listen to the NEVER HAVES
> Then listen close to me—
> Anything can happen, child,
> ANYTHING can be.

From *When Things Fall Apart*
by Pema Chodrön[42]

When things fall apart and we're on the verge of we know not what, the test for each of us is to stay on that brink and not concretize. The spiritual journey is not about heaven and finally getting to a place that's really swell. In fact, that way of looking at things is what keeps us miserable. Thinking that we can find some lasting pleasure and avoid pain is what in Buddhism is called samara, a hopeless cycle that goes round and round endlessly and causes us to suffer greatly. The very first noble truth of the Buddha points out that suffering is inevitable for human beings as long as we believe that things last—that they don't disintegrate, that they can be counted on to satisfy our hunger for security. From this point of view, the only time we know what's really going on is when the rug's pulled out and we can't find anywhere to land. We use these situations either to wake ourselves up or to put ourselves asleep. Right now—in the very instant of groundlessness—is the seed of taking care of those who need our care and of discovering goodness.

I remember so vividly a day in early spring when my whole reality gave out on me. Although it was before I had heard any Buddhist teachings, it was what some would call a genuine spiritual experience. It happened when my husband told me he was having an affair. We lived in northern New Mexico. I was standing in front of our adobe house drinking a cup of tea. I heard the car drive up and the door bang shut. Then he walked around the corner, and without warning he told me that he was having an affair and he wanted a divorce.

I remember the sky and how huge it was. I remember the sound of the river and the steam rising from my tea. There was no time, no thought, there was nothing—just the light and a profound, limitless stillness. Then I regrouped and picked up a stone and threw it at him.

When anyone asks me how I got involved in Buddhism, I always say it was because I was so angry with my husband. The truth is that he saved my life. When that marriage fell apart, I tried hard—very, very hard—to go back to some kind of comfort, some kind of security, some kind of familiar resting place. Fortunately for me, I could never pull it off. Instinctively I knew that annihilation of my old dependent, clinging self was the only way to go.

Life is a good teacher and a good friend. Things are always in transition, if we could only realize it. Nothing ever sums itself up in the way that we like to dream about. The off-center, in-between state is an ideal situation, a situation in which we don't get caught and we can open our hearts and minds beyond limit. It's a very tender, non-aggressive, open-ended state of affairs.

To stay with that shakiness—to stay with a broken heart, with a rumbling stomach, with the feeling of hopelessness and wanting to get revenge—that is the path of true awakening. Sticking with that uncertainty, getting the knack of relaxing in the midst of chaos, learning not to panic—this is the spiritual path. Getting the knack of catching ourselves, of gently and compassionately catching ourselves, is the path of the warrior. We catch ourselves one zillion times as once again, whether we like it or not, we harden into resentment, bitterness, righteous indignation—harden in any way, even into a sense of relief, a sense of inspiration.

Every day, at the moment when things get edgy, we can just ask ourselves, "Am I going to practice peace, or am I going to war?"

SIX

SPEAKING ONE'S TRUTH

And a large crowd followed him and pressed in on him. Now there was a woman who had been suffering from hemorrhages for twelve years. She had endured much under many physicians, and had spent all that she had; and she was no better, but rather grew worse. She had heard about Jesus, and came up behind him in the crowd and touched his cloak, for she said, "If I but touch his clothes, I will be made well." Immediately her hemorrhage stopped; and she felt in her body that she was healed of her disease.

Immediately aware that power had gone forth from him, Jesus turned about in the crowd and said, "Who touched my clothes?"

And his disciples said to him, "You see the crowd pressing in on you; how can you say, 'Who touched me?'"

He looked all around to see who had done it. But the woman, knowing what had happened to her, came in fear and trembling, fell down before him, and told him the whole truth. He said to her, "Daughter, your faith has made you well; go in peace, and be healed of your disease." (Mark 5:24–34)

Reflections
BY CAREN

Billy died fifteen years ago when he was fifteen. Not from an illness or an accident. Billy died because he chose to.

Like all suicides, Billy's was a desolate act of self-annihilation that shocked and confounded his adoptive family, friends, and community into new realities. For Greg, a self-employed businessman who was Billy's youth group leader, a mentor, and a close family friend, the news was particularly devastating. And for the fifteen years that followed Billy's death, he felt as though a part of him died also.

With a posture of sadness that comes from the heart and not the head, from hindsight, not forethought, Greg recalled talking with Billy two weeks before he died. During the conversation, Greg's thoughts turned back seven years to memories of the joy his friends had felt when they adopted Billy. But their joy was short-lived. From the beginning, it seemed that the wily boy was destined to be branded as troubled and a troublemaker. But, Greg thought, no matter how outrageous Billy's behavior became, those who cared always reassured him that he was wanted, loved, and lovable.

Like other close friends, Billy and Greg shared not only talk, but silence, too. Breaking through one of those moments, Billy asked Greg whether or not people who kill themselves go to heaven. Assuming that he was referring to Billy's birth mother's suicide, Greg replied: "The God I worship is a kind and loving God. I'm sure this God wouldn't keep people out of heaven for ending their life if it had been so painful that they just couldn't bear to live it any longer." When Greg felt the answer satisfied Billy, they parted forever.

Contrary to the traditional Western medical model that has dominated our health-care practices since Descartes said, "I think, therefore I am," people in Jesus' time looked at illness holistically. The same is true of native peoples worldwide—not only then, but now. For those viewing illness holistically, disease is *dis*-ease and always a matter of body, mind, and spirit. As indigenous people see it, when one part of our being suffers, the rest of us endures the affliction, too. So their medicine people, known as shamans, give equal weight to a spiritual malaise known as "soul loss." Soul loss—an intangible loss caused by both real and imagined trauma—wreaks havoc in the form of clinical depression, post-traumatic stress, addictions, psychosomatic episodes, and other complaints that can cause people's vitality and deepest connections to their inner and outer worlds to ebb away.

To help ease the intractable pain of Billy's death, Greg gradually gave up working with the youth group and spent the next fifteen years focused on other thoughts and activities. As a cover-up it seemed to mask not only his pain, but his unconscious soul loss, too. That is, until the day a youth leader at his church announced he could not accompany the teenagers on a pilgrimage to Iona, Scotland. Seeing Greg walk by, two teens begged him, "Please come with us. We really need you." Reluctantly, Greg agreed.

Iona is a small island off the northwest coast of Scotland. Every Saturday, pilgrims representing diverse spiritual and religious traditions arrive to spend a week living as individuals in community at a restored eleventh-century abbey. Here, sojourners gather daily with the nondenominational group that runs the abbey to work, eat, pray, and examine and discover self anew.

As he approached the abbey to participate in services for the first time, Greg expected to enter through a doorway but encountered a floodgate instead—one that could no longer hold back fifteen years of unrelenting self-doubts, fears, rebukes, and an abiding guilt that screamed, "You were responsible for Billy's death! You! You gave him permission to die."

The groundswell caused tears long forced underground in the wake of Billy's death to resurface. And as the tide engulfed him at the service, on the moors, and on his pillow, Greg wanted to run from the island, the youth, and his pain. In pondering the possibilities, he turned, instead, in the only direction that felt safe.

Greg met with two priests at the abbey who listened to his story—not just the facts, but "the whole truth" about his anger over Billy's death, his sorrow, his guilt, his inability to forgive, and his questions about his faith. The next morning, while facing east to watch the sunrise over a strait of wind-whipped water, Greg prayed, "God, I think that my soul will always have a scorched place. But that's okay. At least it's mostly clear again. Looking back at the years that I was away from you, I was not a whole person. Something was wrong, but I didn't know what. Thank you from the bottom of my heart for your gifts of healing and grace."

Wanderings and Wonderings

Re-read the scriptural text with curious eyes, and imagine what life might be like for the woman with the hemorrhage as she goes about her day and dreams in the night. Imagine her thoughts and hopes after so many failed attempts to be healed. Study the expressions on her face and touch the feelings in her heart as she leaves her house in a society where purity laws classify women with her condition as "unclean."

Now stand up and be the woman with the flow of blood. Envision yourself in her clothes and her state of physical, emotional, and financial destitution. Be conscious of all your thoughts and feelings as you stand outside the crowd that has gathered around Jesus. When you are ready, walk into the crowd and toward him. Stand behind him and say, "If I but touch his clothes, I will be made well." Then, as you feel the moment to reach out has come at last, touch his clothes.

Take some time to write in your journal or to express in art materials or to ponder, while listening to music, your experience of being this woman. Write a dialogue with her by asking a question, waiting quietly for her reply to break the silence, and then writing down her reply.

The common definition of *hemorrhage* is to bleed profusely or uncontrollably. Another definition is a sudden, uncontrolled, and massive loss of something valuable. Shift gears and use words, phrases, and your imagination to describe what has been happening medically for eighteen years to the woman with a flow of blood. Now think about her condition metaphorically, and consider her daily struggles from that perspective.

The text says that when she touches Jesus' cloak, she stops hemorrhaging and feels healed of her disease.

- Where in your world or across the world do you see people who are willing to break through crowds, institutional barriers, and other obstacles to find, reach out, and connect to a source of healing?
- And in your life, where, when, and how have you yearned for and searched for an unconventional source of healing in the midst of more conventional ones?
  - If found or encountered, what form did it take?
  - Is it one you still return to and/or rely on today?

The climax of the story occurs publicly when "the woman, knowing what had happened to her, came in fear and trembling, fell down before him, and told him the whole truth." We can't know this woman's truth. But you can search for your own.

Write a statement in your journal that expresses your understanding of the phrase "*whole* truth." Begin by pondering truth that comes effortlessly to mind. Now summon up a time when an event or circumstance may have led you or driven you to choose whether or not to dig deeper into all the layers of your truth—the truth of who you are that could no longer be rationalized, justified, or explained away. Finally, ask yourself: What *really* is my truth? The truth that is behind my mask or persona; the truth that exposes places within that have been hidden, buried, disguised, ignored, feared, or kept secret for a long, long time? The truth that contains my deepest, most personal longings, secrets, regrets, desires, dreams, potentials, fears, fantasies, and foibles?

As you recall or relive the details of that time, recapture moments when you felt ambivalent, scared, fearless, cowardly, anxious, and assured as you lived the persistent, annoying, frightening questions about whether or not to face your truth, to consider seeing it anew, and to acknowledge and accept it.

If you chose to peek at, dig into, or attempt to fully expose that whole truth to yourself, recall whether you then decided to disclose it to another.

- If, on one hand, you chose not to tell another, why?
- What resulted from not disclosing your *whole* truth?
- If, on the other hand, you did speak your *whole* truth, how did it impact your relationship with the other?
- Was the cost worth the promise?

Look around your world and name someone living or dead to whom you want to speak the *whole* truth today. List the known consequences—positive and negative—of doing so and of *not* doing so.

At the end of the story, Jesus does not tell the woman that he has made her well. Instead, he tells her that her *faith* has made her well. Re-read the text with open eyes and ears, and be curious about what Jesus may be seeing and hearing when he makes that comment about her faith. Note what he says and does not say.

- How do you understand the relationship between telling one's whole truth, having faith, and being made well?
- And finally, today, where or when do you find yourself in the tension of whether or not to delve into, unearth, and then disclose a *whole* truth that you've closeted and kept safe from exposure—a truth that could become a passage to a healing that awaits you?

Mirrors

The quest for truth . . . is to let suffering speak.
    —Cornel West, *The Cornel West Reader*[43]

Knowing can be a curse on a person's life. I'd traded in a pack of lies for a pack of truth, and I didn't know which one was heavier. Which one took the most strength to carry around? It was a ridiculous question, though, because once you know the truth, you can't ever go back and pick up your suitcase of lies. Heavier or not, the truth is yours now.
    —Sue Monk Kidd, *The Secret Life of Bees*[44]

But if there be truth in me, it should explode. I cannot reject it; I would be rejecting myself.
    —Karol Wojtyla, Pope John Paul II, quoted in *Time*

The best mind-altering drug is truth.

> —Lily Tomlin, from *Healing Words for the Body, Mind, and Spirit: 101 Words to Inspire and Affirm* by Caren Goldman[45]

From *The Kite Runner*
by Khaled Hosseini[46]

"Listen," she said, "I want to tell you something. Something you have to know before . . ."

"I don't care what it is."

"You need to know. I don't want us to start with secrets. And I'd rather you hear it from me."

"If it will make you feel better, tell me. But it won't change anything."

There was a long pause at the other end. . . . "So, does what I told you bother you?"

"A little," I said. I owed her the truth on this one. I couldn't lie to her and say that my pride, my *iftikhar*, wasn't stung at all that she had been with a man, whereas I had never taken a woman to bed. It did bother me a bit, but I had pondered this quite a lot in the weeks before I asked Baba to go *khastegari*. And in the end the question that always came back to me was this: How could I, of all people, chastise someone for their past?

"Does it bother you enough to change your mind?"

"No, Soraya. Not even close," I said. "Nothing you said changes anything. I want us to marry."

She broke into fresh tears.

I envied her. Her secret was out. Spoken. Dealt with. I opened my mouth and almost told her how I'd betrayed Hassan, lied, driven him out, and destroyed a forty-year relationship between Baba and Ali. But I didn't. I suspected there were many ways in which Soraya Taheri was a better person than me. Courage was just one of them. . . .

The connection went through on the fourth try. . . .

"It's me," I said.

"Amir!" she almost screamed. "Are you okay? Where are you?"

"I'm in Pakistan."

"Why didn't you call earlier? I've been sick with *tashweesh*! My mother's praying and doing *mazr* every day."

"I'm sorry I didn't call. I'm fine now." I had told her I'd be away a week, two at the most. I'd been gone for nearly a month. . . .

"What do you mean 'fine now'? And what's wrong with your voice?"

"Don't worry about that for now. I'm fine. Really. Soraya, I have a story to tell you, a story I should have told you a long time ago. . . ."

Then I did what I hadn't done in fifteen years of marriage: I told my wife everything. Everything. I had pictured this moment so many times, dreaded it, but, as I spoke, I felt something lifting off my chest. I imagined Soraya had experienced something very similar the night of our *khaste-gari*, when she'd told me about her past. By the time I was done with my story, she was weeping.

Healing
by D. H. Lawrence[47]

I am not a mechanism, an assembly of various sections.
And it is not because the mechanism is working wrongly, that
  I am ill.
I am ill because of wounds to the soul, to the deep emotional self,
And the wounds to the soul take a long, long time, only time can
  help
And patience, and a certain difficult repentance,
Long, difficult repentance, realization of life's mistake, and the
  freeing oneself
From the endless repetition of the mistake
Which mankind at large has chosen to sanctify.

SEVEN

LOVING WITH ALL

Just then a lawyer stood up to test Jesus. "Teacher," he said, "what must I do to inherit eternal life?"

He said to him, "What is written in the law? What do you read there?"

He answered, "You shall love the Lord your God with all your heart, and with all your soul, and with all your strength, and with all your mind; and your neighbor as yourself."

And he said to him, "You have given the right answer; do this, and you will live." (Luke 10:25–28)

Reflections
BY CAREN

While quietly sitting on the porch of my multicolored, gabled Victorian home, I suddenly decide to fish my mother's mind for the reasons she became an Orthodox Jew after sixty-something years of living the secular life and loving shrimp and lobsters. I begin with a baited question about an ancient Hebrew prayer known as the *Sh'ma* to entice this five-foot, ninety-pound, seventy-something great-grandmother into a conversation destined to last the afternoon. "It's the most important prayer for Jews everywhere," I say with a confidence that comes from a lifetime of knowing that truth. "But what does it really mean for you to love God with *all* your heart, soul, and mind?"

Discerning that I'm not casually trolling around her heart and soul but deliberately probing her mind with a barbed hook, my mother smiles and takes a diversionary tack. She, who usually tells me how to build a clock when all I've asked for is the time, sits in silence. As moments become long minutes, I'm lured into believing her answer will fill volumes. At last words come. "Why do you ask?"

If I were completely honest, I would answer: "Mom, I think I know what you're going to say, but it's not what I really want to hear." Instead, I reply with a half-truth that warns her that I'm out to catch her but to do no harm. She, in turn, knows that whenever this familiar outing ends, she will be gently released. Of course I, in a state of lingering adolescent arrogance, determine that from this point on I will not be hooked by other silences.

"Late in life you decided that your God—our God—was a God worthy of your time, energy, devotion, heart, mind, soul, strength, and kosher kitchen. I need to understand how you got there."

"What's to understand?" she questions in a way that assures me that she, not I, will answer. "It's very clear," she continues. "The *Sh'ma* says to love God with all your heart, mind, and soul. So I do. I go to *shul* [synagogue], I keep the Sabbath, I keep kosher, I study Torah, and . . . Look, I just don't keep this and do that like I'm spinning a wheel and each time it comes around say, 'There, God, I keep and do so that means I love you.' What I keep and what I do is done with love and respect in my heart."

Her words entice me. I know she means what she says, but I decide to risk rocking the boat anyhow. "I know everything you do to please God is done with love in your heart. But the commandment is to love God with *all* your heart. Tell me about *all* your heart. Tell me about *all* your mind. Tell me about *all* your soul."

Poet Robert Bly often writes about our shadow side. He likens this constant companion or alter ego to a long black bag that we drag behind us. In my case I imagine an unwieldy sack stuffed with disenfranchised parts of my mind, body, and spirit. Whenever I rummage around in that sack, I realize that most of the contents resemble my thoughts, emotions, attitudes, feelings, actions, deeds, body parts, and projections on others. On closer examination I'm apt to note that some of the contents of the sack actually look like "good" qualities—but in others' eyes, not in mine. For me it's best that whatever has been allocated to the bag is kept secret and in the dark. Every time I look in this bag, I sigh because it's so heavy—a burden that weighs me down—and so I want to give it away instead of owning all of who I was and who I am. However, when in a default mode, I realize that most of the time I don't have to look in the sack at all unless I really want to. That's because this bag, like my back, is behind me, and without a mirror to remind me it's there, I can always pretend it doesn't exist.

That afternoon as my mother allowed me to peek into her sack of sorrows, regrets, shattered dreams, and betrayals, I realized how many times she must have crawled into that dark, messy abyss during her attempts to love God with all. I asked if she took those forays when deciding to give up her addictions, self-hatred, and abiding resentment of those who had hurt her in the past, and she said, "Yes." I also asked if it was such rummaging that allowed her to finally reconnect with her grandchildren and me after years of unexplained silence. "Yes." But I didn't have to ask if she looked from the inside out on the day she realized that only she could accept or reject all that comprised her burdensome load. Looking into her teary eyes as she took my hands in hers, raised them to her lips, gave them a kiss, and pressed them to her cheek, I knew the answer.

I know my faithful Jewish mother of blessed memory would probably roll her eyes at the thought of me quoting a Christian saint in a discussion of the *Sh'ma*. "What's the matter—aren't there enough good rabbis to make your point?" she'd ask.

"Of course there are," I'd say to appease her before throwing out a line. "However, some of the rabbis I know quote saints, too—saints like Francis of Assisi, who said, 'Love the leper inside.'"

Wanderings and Wonderings

"Just then a lawyer stood up to test Jesus. 'Teacher,' he said, 'what must I do to inherit eternal life?'"

In this exchange between Jesus and the lawyer, the gospel writer chose his words and characters carefully. Think about the lawyer. If he knows nothing else, he does know the law. So why a test? To see whether or not Jesus knows the law? To uncover hidden truth? Or for some other reason? Next, mull over the broader implications of the lawyer's question. Begin by contemplating what it means to inherit something, what kinds of things we inherit, and how inheritances happen. List items, characteristics, attitudes, and legacies that you have already inherited in your lifetime, as well as those things you hope or plan to inherit someday. Also ponder the phrase "eternal life"—your own understanding of those words as well as others' explanations and definitions. Now, in your own words, say or write what you believe the lawyer is asking—what he really wants to know.

Interestingly, Jesus replies not with an answer but with another question. In response, the lawyer references the *Sh'ma*, ancient words from Deuteronomy that express a core tenet of Jewish people. According to

Rabbi Joseph Telushkin, "Although Judaism has no catechism, the biblical verse '*Sh'ma Yisrael, Adonai Eloheinu, Adonai Edhad*—Hear, O Israel, the Lord is our God, the Lord is One' comes closest to being Judaism's credo."[48] When Jews recite the *Sh'ma* three times daily, the six opening words are followed by text that contains the first part of the lawyer's response.

> Hear, O Israel: the Lord is our God, the Lord is One.
> Blessed be His Name whose glorious kingdom is forever and ever.
> And thou shall love the LORD your God with all your heart,
> and with all your soul,
> and with all your might.
> And these words, which I command thee this day,
> shall be upon your heart,
> and thou shall teach them diligently unto your children;
> and shall talk of them
> when thou sit in your house
> and when thou walk by the way
> and when thou lie down, and when thou rise up.
> And thou shall bind them for a sign upon your hand,
> and they shall be for frontlets between your eyes.
> And thou shall write them upon the door-posts of your house
> and upon your gates.[49]

"You shall love the Lord your God with all your heart, and with all your soul, and with all your strength, and with all your mind."
    Look up the word *all* in a dictionary and a thesaurus and then ask yourself:

- What do I know about the heart? *All* my heart?
- What can I say about *all* my soul?
- *All* my strength—what does that refer to?
- And what might the word *all* mean when it comes to my mind?

God commanded Moses, the wandering Jews in the desert, and every generation to follow to love with *all*.

- Why do you think God wants and values *all*?
- And the word *love*—why might God choose the verb *love* instead of *respect, obey, submit, follow, defer,* or *comply*?
- In what ways do we demonstrate what it means *not* to love?

Write the equation "loving with all =" on a piece of paper. Now fill in what one is required to do without using the word *love*.

In this encounter, Jesus affirms the lawyer's answer. Reflect on your whole heart, your whole mind, your whole soul, and your whole strength.

- Which of these parts do you rely on the most?
- The least?
- Which have you loved with?
- Which do you love with the best?

Consider the next admonition: *"and your neighbor as yourself."*

- Can you describe what happens when you love your neighbor with all but love yourself with less than all?

The sequence is heart, strength, soul, and mind, and then neighbor as yourself. However, the *Sh'ma* doesn't begin with the words "you shall." Instead, it begins with, "Hear, O Israel." Many scholars consider a new translation of the Torah by Emmett Fox to be closest to the original Hebrew. Fox's prelude to the *Sh'ma* is "Hearken, O Israel: YHWH our God, YHWH (is) One!" Note that this means not merely that there is one God, but that God is whole, complete, perfect: One. Contemplate the differences between having one God and having a God who is One, and consider the ways in which each description impacts your understanding of the *Sh'ma* and what God wants from each of us.

Write the words to the *Sh'ma* in your journal and personalize the lawyer's response to Jesus by changing the words *you* and *your* to *I* and *my*. Say this version aloud several times, and then listen to what the voices in your head and, perhaps, your heart, may be saying or asking. Question those voices; ask them, how might the ways I love myself be related to the ways I love others and God?

Finally, wonder what Jesus may have meant by the word *live*. Then, using words, art materials, a musical instrument, and/or body movement, express your response to the question, what is the life *I* want?

Mirrors

God calls us to take the path of the inner truth—and that means taking responsibility for "everything" that's in you: for what pleases you and for what you're ashamed of. In the spiritual life, nothing goes away. There is no heavenly garbage dump. It's all here, wherever we are. Everything belongs.
—Richard Rohr, *Quest for the Grail*[50]

Is the life I'm living the life that wants to live in me?
> —Parker Palmer, from *I Will Not Die an Unlived Life*
>   by Dawna Markova[51]

> It's the heart afraid of breaking that never learns to dance.
> It's the dream afraid of waking that never takes the chance.
> It's the one who won't be taken, who cannot seem to give,
> and the soul afraid of dyin' that never learns to live.
> > —Manda McBroom, from *Healing Words for the Body,*
> >   *Mind and Spirit* by Caren Goldman[52]

My fullest concentration of energy is available to me only when I integrate all the parts of who I am, openly, allowing power from particular sources of my living to flow back and forth freely through all my different selves, without restrictions of externally imposed definition. Only then can I bring myself and my energies as a whole to the service of those struggles which I embrace as part of my living.
> —Audre Lorde, *Sister Outsider: Essays and Speeches*[53]

Heart Prayer
by Elizabeth Cunningham[54]

> You can only pray what's in your heart.
>
> So if your heart is being ripped from your chest
> pray the tearing
>
> if your heart is full of bitterness
> pray it to the last dreg
>
> if your heart is a river gone wild
> pray the torrent
>
> or a lava flow scorching the mountain
> pray the fire
>
> pray the scream in your heart
> the fanning bellows
>
> pray the rage, the murder
> and the mourning
>
> pray your heart into the great quiet hands that can hold it
> like the small bird it is.

The Clay Jug
by Kabir[55]

Inside this clay jug there are canyons and pine
    mountains, and the maker of canyons and pine
    mountains!
All seven oceans are inside, and hundreds of millions of
    stars.
The acid that tests gold is there, and the one who judges
    jewels.
And the music from the strings no one touches, and the
    source of all water.

If you want the truth, I will tell you the truth:
Friend, listen: the God whom I love is inside.

EIGHT

STANDING UP STRAIGHT

Now he was teaching in one of the synagogues on the sabbath. And just then there appeared a woman with a spirit that had crippled her for eighteen years. She was bent over and was quite unable to stand up straight. When Jesus saw her, he called her over and said, "Woman, you are set free from your ailment." When he laid his hands on her, immediately she stood up straight and began praising God. But the leader of the synagogue, indignant because Jesus had cured on the sabbath, kept saying to the crowd, "There are six days on which work ought to be done; come on those days and be cured, and not on the sabbath day." But the Lord answered him and said, "You hypocrites! Does not each of you on the sabbath untie his ox or his donkey from the manger, and lead it away to give it water? And ought not this woman, a daughter of Abraham whom Satan bound for eighteen long years, be set free from this bondage on the sabbath day?" When he said this, all his opponents were put to shame; and the entire crowd was rejoicing at all the wonderful things that he was doing. (Luke 13:10–17)

Reflections
BY BILL

Readers of Mary Oliver's poetry are familiar with her images of walking the beach to gather seashells. Remnants of a whelk, a broken clam, and a scarred barnacle, she suggests, are like little words that tell us of broken parts of our lives. "Then you begin, slowly," Oliver writes at the end of her poem "Breakage," "to read the whole story."

Each of our lives, made up of countless broken pieces, can come together in more than one way to tell our story. It is on those rare occasions, when we dare to tell ourselves one of the many versions of that life story, that we may find the courage to stand up straight and face the world as we are—without excuse or blame.

Such a moment came in my early forties while visiting a lovely suburban parish in St. Louis that was searching for a new minister. Before the tour of the church ended, I knew it was a not a job for me. Late in the afternoon, as a meeting with the calling committee drew to a close, a committee member who had been silent throughout the meeting said that he had one more question. Turning to me with the hint of a sardonic smile, he asked, "Can you tell us, Mr. Dols, why you chose to become ordained?" There was a hook hidden somewhere in the request, and I could feel its barb. I thought to myself, "Why not tell him?" I paused, took a deep breath, and told him about growing up in Baltimore and my dreams of attending the United States Naval Academy in nearby Annapolis. By my mid-teens, however, my eyesight had failed; in those days, my need for glasses disqualified me. So plan B, my mother told me, was to go to seminary and become a minister. "They will take good care of you," she said.

After people around the table laughed, as have others during the countless times I have told the same story over the years, the room became quiet as the man who asked me the question said, "You know, some mothers are very wise." Immediately, it dawned on me that after nearly twenty years I had finally found the missing broken shell, the hidden puzzle piece that completed one important version of my life story.

My mother was, indeed, very wise. For perhaps the first time, I knew— I could not deny—that my successful, comfortable, secure, and safe career in the church had from the start been part of a yearning to be taken care of and shielded from some of the demands and requirements of a world that frightened me. I knew in my gut that while doing some of the best and most loving things in the world, I had, at the same time, used the church to hide from a kind of growing up—a maturing that I longed for yet feared. The memory of that meeting with the St. Louis parish still haunts me, still reminds me how years of hard work and soul-searching can also, and unknowingly, be a subtle form of gentle bondage.

One thing this version of my life story explains to me is a style of ministry and life marked by an enduring need to test boundaries and go to the frontier. From the beginning of seminary, I had little tolerance for rigid orthodox theologies that boxed God into creeds, catechisms, and liturgies.

I lived most of my days in small groups seeking religious insight in novels, drama, and poetry. I was more interested in how God could be engaged than understood, more committed to exploring human potential than seeking doctrinal correctness. Early on I began a psychological journey that led me through endless hours of therapy and a sabbatical that might have become a road out of the church into ministry as a pastoral counselor. I pushed and stretched, not always sure what the missing piece was but still determined I would live, as Auntie Mame exhorted, a "three-dimensional life . . . soaking up life down to your toes!" Protected by my clerical collar, I entered the civil rights struggle in Wilmington, North Carolina, and joined battles around Prayer Book revisions and the ordination of women in the Episcopal Church. The urge was always toward growing rather than believing. I was hungry for the possible *more* in my life and the world, to which I kept hearing Jesus call me.

At the age of fifty, after twenty-five years in the parish ministry, I drove a rental truck out of the church lot in Alexandria one morning in 1983 and headed across the continent to California. A good friend told me to associate quickly with a parish when I arrived or, he warned, "You're going to drift." I drifted. Through four years of graduate school, I drifted in and out of classes and seminars and every place but back to the institutional church. In Berkeley on my four-year "sabbatical," I knew, as I had at last known that afternoon in St. Louis, that my creative if sometimes angry, irrational, and irascible behavior as a priest was an effort to break out of my bondage, stand up straight, and finally grow up.

When I returned to a church community six years before retirement, I served an extraordinary congregation of Baptists in Charlotte, North Carolina. Having learned by then some important things about Jesus, about the church, about what it means to be religious and human, and most of all about myself, I was no longer bent over and weighed down by a role and institution that began as a refuge but had become a convenient excuse for life. I was no longer quite so bent out of shape. I was ready to stand up and face the world.

Many of us are bent over, weighed down, invisibly bound in ways that keep us safe and secure but rob us of life. Being called to a career, relationship, addiction, lifestyle, or even religious conviction can come from the depths of fear and anxiety that drive us, or gently lead us, to lives that look enviable and enjoyable while they bend us over and even break us. For some of us it is not until we get close to the end of our story—sometimes, even, the final chapter—that the truth is unveiled and we set ourselves free.

Wanderings and Wonderings

Think about this woman who has been bent over for eighteen years, and envision how she looks. Moreover, imagine life for her in a patriarchal society governed by purity codes. In such a culture, infirmities are believed to be a consequence of sinning—violating God's law. With that in mind, consider what you know about how people with physical and mental conditions are treated in other Bible stories, and wonder about this woman's relationships with and to others in her family and community.

Stand up, take a deep breath, bend over as far as you can, and walk around the room as she might. Be aware of what your body tells you about your worldview and living life as a bent-over one.

Then as the bent-over woman, stand up straight, look around, and observe what happens to you and your world. Identify thoughts, feelings, and perspectives that shift, suddenly, on being set free. Pinpoint promises and dreams now possible after the past eighteen years. Also contemplate and anticipate new fears and anxieties that may be born as a result of your healing. On one side of a page, list what this woman may gain from being healed. On the other side, list what she may have to give up. Now ponder these questions:

- "A spirit of infirmity"—how would you describe it?
- What do you suppose Jesus sees when he looks at the bent-over woman with a spirit of infirmity?
- Does he perceive something about her that others might miss?

Though she has not sought him out, asks nothing of him, and does not request healing or mention repentance, Jesus calls her over and announces that she is set free from her ailment. When he lays hands on her, she stands up straight and praises God.

- What is going on between Jesus and the unnamed woman?
- What does calling this woman over in the synagogue and touching her on the Sabbath say to you about Jesus?

The synagogue leader speaks up.

- What do you speculate about a man in such a position of religious authority?

He is indignant.

- What does it mean to experience "indignation"?
- Where in this man's deep sense of responsibility, or in his anxieties and fears, might this indignation reside?

Nowhere else in Scripture is a woman called "a daughter of Abraham." Hear the crowd talking among themselves as Jesus calls her "a daughter of Abraham." Wonder, too, about the synagogue leader's reaction and the woman's.

Look at the evening news or around your office, classroom, congregation, grocery store, or kitchen table, and see bent-over ones in the world today.

- What bends them out of shape and weighs them down?
- Who *really* sees them?
- To whom are they invisible?
- Flaunting authority, who calls them over, announces they are free, and then touches and empowers them to stand up straight?
- Where are the indignant voices of authority you hear saying "not today" or "not in this place" located?
- How do the indignant ones in your communities, institutions, and even your family forbid the crossing of certain boundaries, calling it unlawful and unacceptable?

Stand in front of a mirror and be bent over, weighed down, bound, and not free.

- Who or what in your life is bending you over?
- Name a part of your life that is dying to stand up straight.
- Uninvited and even unsought, who—from afar or from deep within— is calling you to move toward healing?
- Who, in your outer world and/or your psyche and soul, are the "synagogue leaders" telling you, "Nobody gets it all," "Be glad you have what you've got," "If you had only listened to me," and "What will people think"?
- Who is your inner synagogue leader, that keeper of order, law, decorum, boundaries, and good sense, who is necessary and helpful but who responds with fear when another inner voice coaxes you toward freedom and beckons you to stand up straight?

Mull over choices you may be making every day to stay in comfortable bondage rather than brave the bewildering possibilities and the new challenges that you would face—and embrace—if you were unbound, set free, and able to finally stand up straight.

Mirrors

It is tragic how few people ever "possess their souls" before they die. "Nothing is more rare in any man," says Emerson, "than an act of his own." It is quite true. Most people are other people. Their thoughts are someone else's opinions, their lives a mimicry, their passions a quotation.
   —Oscar Wilde, *The Portable Oscar Wilde*[56]

   What's best in me lives underground.
   Rooting and digging, itching for wings.
      —Stanley Kunitz, "The Mound Builders," in *The Collected Poems*[57]

In order to lift your voice, you have to lift your head.
   —Maya Angelou, *I Know Why the Caged Bird Sings*[58]

Sometimes you got the feeling when you met someone—the horizon widened. Most of the time, after you got to know the person, the widening feeling went away. You got used to the person's vista. But with Kay the feeling had lasted. In his better moments he could believe that with her, he might become the person he wanted to be. Then he would review all that would have to change and it would look impossible.
   —Susan Minot, *Rapture*[59]

Turn Over Your Hand
by William Stafford[60]

   Those lines on your palm, they can be read
   for a hidden part of your life that only
   those links can say—nobody's voice
   can find so tiny a message as comes
   across your hand. Forbidden to complain,
   you have tried to be like somebody else,
   and only this fine record you examine
   sometimes like this can remember where
   you were going before that long
   silent evasion that your life became.

God Says Yes to Me
by Kaylin Haught[61]

I asked God if it was okay to be melodramatic
and she said yes
I asked her if it was okay to be short
and she said it sure is
I asked her if I could wear nail polish
or not wear nail polish
and she said honey
she calls me that sometimes
she said you can do just exactly
what you want to
Thanks God I said
And is it even okay if I don't paragraph
my letters
Sweetcakes God said
who knows where she picked that up
what I'm telling you is
Yes Yes Yes

NINE

BINDING WOUNDS

Jesus [said], "A man was going down from Jerusalem to Jericho, and fell into the hands of robbers, who stripped him, beat him, and went away, leaving him half dead. Now by chance a priest was going down that road; and when he saw him, he passed by on the other side. So likewise a Levite, when he came to the place and saw him, he passed by on the other side. But a Samaritan while traveling came near him; and when he saw him, he was moved with pity. He went to him and bandaged his wounds, having poured oil and wine on them.

Then he put him on his own animal, brought him to an inn, and took care of him. The next day he took out two denarii, gave them to the innkeeper, and said, 'Take care of him; and when I come back, I will repay you whatever more you spend.'" (Luke 10:30–35)

Reflections
BY CAREN

It's the summer of 1998, and my seventy-four-year-old mother, Muriel, has joined me for a much too short weekend visit. As we watch the sunrise from the deck of my vacation home in the mountains of West Virginia, I look at this stranger I've known my whole life and listen carefully as she begins reading aloud from memory the gray chapters of her life. Watching her blond pageboy haircut bob as she restructures old stories, laughs at foibles past, tears up as enduring pain resurfaces, and searches for the strings that tie them all together, I notice that I tilt my head the same way she does when speaking.

Through most of her journey, Muriel frequented roads littered with the debris of being an unloved, unwanted child—a Cinderella who would never go to the ball. From birth her parents told her, "You're a mistake," and throughout childhood she endured other psychological abuse that left festering wounds and the odd feeling that she was her own best enemy.

When Muriel graduated from high school at age fifteen, teachers urged her parents to send their brilliant one to college. "No," they replied. "Why waste good money?" So Muriel worked in a department store to pay for her room and board instead. Soon after her seventeenth birthday, a girl-friend introduced her to Bernie—five years her senior and often mistaken for Frank Sinatra. The woeful themes of their shared stories resonated, and the smitten couple felt like soul mates. Desperate for attention, love, and acceptance, each wanted nothing more than to heroically rescue the other. "This is what love feels like. This is what love looks like," they told themselves before saying "Yes!" to marriage.

However, after ten years of broken vows driven by Bernie's narcissism, distrust, and dark depression, Muriel awakened to the reality that her Prince Charming might be Darth Vader. Psychological and physical abuse, rage, disconnection, and scapegoating recapitulated lifelong humiliations in her heart, psyche, and soul: "You are unlovable! You're of no use. You're responsible for others' misery."

One day, feeling emotionally and physically abandoned, experiencing the familiar tug of being an enemy of her own kin and chained on a path going nowhere, Muriel heard an inner voice. Over and over it convinc-ingly suggested alcohol, mind-altering drugs, anorexia, bulimia, and sui-cide as ways to travel elsewhere and escape. Muriel listened and tried them all during long, despondent nights at the bottom of her soul, until one morning while lying in bed, she dreamed that she was holding a dead child in her arms and crying. Suddenly she screamed at the child, "Wake up!" and the child did. So did my mother. For the first time in twenty years, she decided to stop beating herself up and feeling robbed of her worth. Moments later, she walked into the kitchen, stood before my father, and demanded a divorce.

Free at last, but alone and frightened by an unknown future and the prospect of being a single parent, Muriel journeyed forward to a Promised Land. Once on that road, she took classes at the community college and began dating a new friend named Bill.

Empowered by Bill's devotion, encouragement, and tender binding of her festering wounds, Muriel felt as though she could, at last, be lovable. Two years later they married, and she continued to blossom. When we vis-ited, she no longer faded into a locked bedroom for days at a time. But

when Bill died two years later during heart surgery, Muriel's world shattered. Once again she found herself cast into Dante's inferno:

> In the middle of our life journey I found
> myself in a dark wood. I had wandered
> from the straight path. It isn't easy to
> talk about it: it was such a thick, wild,
> and rough forest that when I think of it
> my fear returns. . . .

To risk another journey—on a road never taken—would take ten years.
"What changed?" I asked.

"Two things," Muriel recalled. "First, your sister entrusted me with her
newborn son while she worked. I realized I needed to control myself if I
were to care for this fragile new life. Each time I fed him, held him, and
felt his pure heart beating against mine, I discovered more about my self-
loathing and the desire to be loving and kind. During that time, I kept saying 'Thank God' so often that I felt I really should. The next thing I knew I
was attending a synagogue on Shabbot."

Muriel's story could end there. But it doesn't. She not only returned to
her Jewish roots; she also dug deeper into smelly muck to ensure that her
tree of life would never again wither and dry up. Binding her wounds and
carrying herself to healing places also meant keeping kosher and studying
Torah. When neighbors ailed, Muriel made them chicken soup and per-
formed other kindnesses. She asked nothing in return. On Friday nights,
she observed and embraced the beginning of Sabbath by lighting candles,
saying prayers, and breaking bread. She even risked sipping ritual wine.
"First a battle not to drink the whole bottle. Then a pleasure, thank God,
to not be my bitterest enemy and to be in control."

From sundown to sundown on Friday and Saturday, Muriel lived and
loved Jewish law on a clearly defined path. She wouldn't write, cook, flick a
light switch, or drive. She would walk to her Orthodox synagogue with new
friends and return home to sit with her cat, thoughts, plants, prayers, and
Torah. And she would, at last, smile and feel pleasing to herself and God.

In the years since my mother's death, I think about her daily. Each time
I see her as the wounded healer of her life story—no longer beating herself up on roads named victimization, self-pity, hatred, degradation, and
despair. No longer being robbed of self-worth, feeling half dead, and
watching the world go by, but traveling healing paths and leaving a legacy
of compassion, generosity, and loving-kindness behind.

Wonderings and Wanderings

Allow yourself to read the Good Samaritan parable as though you were encountering it for the very first time. Try reading it aloud so you can hear the words and phrases anew. As you do, notice what the story tells you about each of the characters. Take note of information about them that is missing.

Like all parables, this one leaves blanks for you to fill in. However, we do know a few things. For example, in those days, as now, the road from Jerusalem to Jericho passed through deserted areas. "Samaritans were actively persecuting and harassing Jewish pilgrims," says biblical scholar Amy-Jill Levine.[62] Other scholars agree, noting that concern for one's well-being and life was just one reason people often traveled with partners or in caravans. Priests and Levites from other cities, who rotated periods of service in the Temple in Jerusalem and were part of the established religious order, would have been among those travelers. That made the road from Jerusalem to Jericho a popular route.

Then there were the Samaritans. Biblical scholars report that their history goes back to the days following Solomon's reign, when the united empire split. Ten of the twelve Jewish tribes became a kingdom in the north called Israel. The two remaining became the kingdom called Judah (later Judea) in the south. In 722 BCE, the Assyrians occupied and destroyed Israel. Afterward, the Assyrians moved part of the native population out and shifted people from elsewhere in the Middle East in. The mixed inhabitants took their name from Samaria, the capital of the northern kingdom, and became known as the Samaritans. They practiced an Israelite religion, adopted their own version of the five books of Moses as their Bible, and built their own temple on Mount Gerizim in the fourth century BCE. In the first century BCE, John Hyreanus, king of Judah, destroyed Samaria. It was rebuilt by Herod the Great about 30 BCE, and according to Amy-Jill Levine, the Samaritans' culture in Jesus' time rivaled that of the Jews. The two groups abhorred one another so much that in those days calling a Samaritan "good" would be an oxymoron for a Jew. "It would be like saying 'good Nazi.'"[63]

Jesus reports that the priest, Levite, and Samaritan each see the wounded man. But only the Samaritan sees him up close and feels moved by pity. Synonyms for *pity* include *compassion, sympathy, mercy, kindness, forgiveness,* and *understanding.* Another is *shame.*

- What do you imagine that each of the characters really sees? Does not see?
- The gospel tells us that the traveler was "half dead." When you read or hear the expression "half dead," what comes to mind?

Stand up, step into this story, and one by one become the characters. Try making sounds or moving about in ways that help you view them from new perspectives in your outer and your inner worlds.

Be the unidentified man, and as you walk down the road from Jerusalem to Jericho, imagine robbers beating you, stripping you, and leaving you half dead. Then, lying half dead in a roadside ditch, be aware of the priest approaching and walking by. Be aware of the Levite coming your way and passing. And then be aware that another is nearby and that this other stops, sees you, and comes over. Let your thoughts and feelings rise as you realize that this stranger approaching you, touching you, and then binding your wounds is a Samaritan.

- Next, be one of the robbers and strip the man, beat him, and leave him half dead.
- Be the priest. When you see the beaten one, pass him by.
- Be the Levite, see the beaten man, and pass by.
- Finally, be the Samaritan and draw near to the wounded man. When you see him, be moved by pity.
- Now be still and reflect on which characters you identified with the most and the least.

Begin to deepen your experience of this story by imagining that you are a first-century Jew listening to Jesus as he tells it. Tune in to the silent rationales and excuses the religious ones, the establishment, and the authorities make for walking by the robbed and beaten one on the side of the road. Think of reasons why the Samaritan—the enemy, the stranger, and the despised one—chooses to draw near.

Look around your house and out the window and see those in your families, neighborhoods, cities, and elsewhere who are beaten, stripped, robbed, and left half dead.

- Who does the beating?
- What are they stripped and robbed of?
- In what ways are they left half dead?
- Is there a difference between being half dead and being half alive?

Although the thought of walking by beaten, robbed, and half-dead ones in the world around us may be uncomfortable, summon a time when you intentionally or unintentionally did that. Dredge up your thoughts and feelings back then.

Also remember a time when you drew near to someone in dire straits.

- As you got closer, what did you see that you could not see from a distance?
- Did your feelings change when you drew near?
- Did you help the person on the spot?
- Are you aware of the outcome of your choice to help or not to help?

In addition, call to mind a time in your life when you felt robbed, stripped, beaten, and abandoned. See those in your family, neighborhood, country, world, or inside your body, psyche, and soul who threatened your vitality—your life.

- Who were the authorities—religious, political, educational, professional, parental, living or dead—who walked by?
- And who or what symbol of a "Samaritan" who is outside or within your psyche and soul drew near, felt pity, and then cleansed your wounds, carried you to safety, and possibly even offered a hospitable place for you to rest?

Identify an actual road—or an interior one—that you travel daily, weekly, annually, or perhaps for the first time. See the "violent" ones on that road—those who intentionally beat you; rob you of your time, energy, livelihood, relationships, creativity, health, or life-force; and leave you feeling wounded, helpless, and half dead.

- Can you name thoughts, attitudes, fears, prohibitions, inner voices, rules, projections, rejections, or other issues that allow those thieves and muggers to have so much power and *dis*-able you? As you think about those robberies and beatings, name places and times where you can recall robbing yourself and beating yourself up.
- Of what were you robbed?
- Who or what caused you to do that?
- What did you lose in the process?
- Where did you feel most wounded?

Now look around your office, place of worship, neighborhood, or even your family.

- Who, among those you observe, might symbolize the Samaritan in your worldview—the one you despise, reject, and even hate?

- From what, or where in you, do those negative thoughts, feelings, and attitudes originate?
- In what ways do you deliberately avoid, marginalize, and ignore these alien ones?
- Where—around you as well as within you—does this hated, despised, distant, and life-threatening one lurk?

Imagine what your Samaritan—the one deep within who feels condemned by your inner authorities and remains banished by your fears, anxieties, and insecurities—might be waiting patiently to say to you. Moreover, ask yourself, is there something that I need to know that only this Samaritan can tell me?

Also ask yourself, is there a healing from my wounds, pain, trauma, and hatred that can come from no one else?

Continue to mull over questions raised by the story of the Samaritan, and wonder why Jesus told this parable and how might he have come to know this story. Ask yourself, in what ways do I struggle with the reality that this is a story that is alive in the world around me, in my life, and within my psyche, heart, and soul?

It occurs to me how often the decision to help or not to help has less to do with the disposition of our hearts than with the controversy of voices in our heads.
—Garrett Keizer, *Help*[64]

Whoever saves one life saves the entire world.
—The Talmud, *Mishnah Sanhedrin* 4:5

There is nothing heavier than compassion. Not even one's own pain weighs so heavy as the pain one feels with someone, for someone, a pain intensified by the imagination and prolonged by a hundred echoes.
—Milan Kundera, from *The Columbia Dictionary of Quotations*[65]

From *Radical Hospitality*
by Daniel Homan[66]

When we speak of hospitality we are always addressing issues of inclusion and exclusion. Each of us makes choices about who will and who will not be included in our lives. To make such choices is inevitable; we do not have time to be everyone's best friend. The reasons we include and exclude are very personal. You and I probably can't even say why we become close to some people and have no interest in getting to know, or include, others. We only know that we prefer some, and others are harder to like.

Issues of inclusion and exclusion, while personal, are not just personal. Our entire culture excludes many people. If you are in a wheelchair, for example, you are excluded because there are places you can't go. If you are very young, if you are very old, you are excluded. In high school you can be excluded if you don't wear the right shoes or listen to the right music. Women are excluded, as are people of color, and those who practice a religion different from our own.

In our idealism about American life the poor are always excluded; they are our embarrassing little American secret. The American dream has failed the one in six children living in poverty. These children will, most likely, grow up to a lifetime of exclusion. Somewhere, sometime, you were excluded. Remember what that was like. Some people live with the experience constantly.

There was a common saying in Germany just before the Nazi reign: "The human body contains a sufficient amount of fat to make seven cakes of soap, enough iron to make a medium-sized nail, a sufficient amount of phosphorus for two thousand match-heads, enough sulfur to rid one person of fleas." The Nazi view of humanity reduced us to nothing more than the usefulness of our physical components, and when that was used up it was fine to cast aside the human being.

But you and I are much more than what we appear to be. We are more than what we do. We are more than a social or economic class. In the movie *Elephant Man*, actor John Merrick is chased through a train station and cornered in a bathroom by a mob who see only his deformity, his difference from them. He cries out, "I am not an animal. . . . I am a human being. . . ."

This is the sound of every single human heart. It is the cry we make against all that would make us less human, the cry of the darkest night of our lives, the cry of the abandoned and the misunderstood and the excluded. "I am not an animal. I am like you. I am human."

I am not a street person.
I am not a token of my race or creed.
I am not a statistic.
I am not a divorcee.
I am not an AIDS patient.
I am not a sex object.
I am not a laborer
I am not an "at-risk" kid.
I have a mind. I have a heart. I have a soul. I dream. I feel. I care. I am a human being. . . .

In a 1982 report, one ethicist put it this way: "the opposite of cruelty is not simply freedom from the cruel relationship, it is hospitality."

Love after Love
by Derek Walcott[67]

> The time will come
> when, with elation,
> you will greet yourself arriving
> at your own door, in your own mirror,
> and each will smile at the other's welcome,
>
> and say, sit here. Eat.
> You will love again the stranger who was your self.
> Give wine. Give bread. Give back your heart
> to itself, to the stranger who has loved you
>
> all your life, whom you ignored
> for another, who knows you by heart.
> Take down the love letters from the bookshelf,
>
> the photographs, the desperate notes,
> peel your own image from the mirror.
> Sit. Feast on your life.

TEN

CROSSING BOUNDARIES

Jesus left that place and went away to the district of Tyre and Sidon. Just then a Canaanite woman from that region came out and started shouting, "Have mercy on me, Lord, Son of David; my daughter is tormented by a demon." But he did not answer her at all. And his disciples came and urged him, saying, "Send her away, for she keeps shouting after us." He answered, "I was sent only to the lost sheep of the house of Israel." But she came and knelt before him, saying, "Lord, help me." He answered, "It is not fair to take the children's food and throw it to the dogs." She said, "Yes, Lord, yet even the dogs eat the crumbs that fall from their masters' table." Then Jesus answered her, "Woman, great is your faith! Let it be done for you as you wish." And her daughter was healed instantly. After Jesus had left that place, he passed along the Sea of Galilee, and he went up the mountain, where he sat down. (Matthew 15:21–29)

Reflections
BY BILL

I had just driven into the parking lot of the church in Baltimore when I learned I needed to return to George Washington Hospital at once. It had been three days since Shirley had given birth to our third child and first son. Consumed with worry about his respiratory problems, we had yet to agree on his name. I was doing eighty miles per hour on the Baltimore-Washington Parkway, looking hopefully for the policeman who finally pulled me over and then, with red lights blinking, led me through the city. When I arrived at the hospital, I met Dr. Ruth White, our pediatrician, who told me that she had only moments earlier baptized the baby "Jonathan" before he died.

I was devastated, and so was Shirley. In years to come our two daughters, Katherine and Jennifer, would more than fill our lives, but now there was a hole. Not only from our son's death, but from learning that after his traumatic delivery there could be no more pregnancies. Family and friends held and hugged us and said the kind of things people say rather than let the silence and tears be. They said things about God because they had to bring God into it. For the first time in my life, I was face-to-face with death and none of the familiar words fitted or worked. I was told that God chose to have Jonathan with him rather than stay with those of us who would one day be reunited with him. I was told that God needed another angel. I was told that it is all part of God's plan even though we don't know exactly what that is, and that God is in control of the world and that everything happens for the best. None of that computed, and nothing I'd learned in seminary offered any comfort. There were no words that made any sense out of the aching nonsense of my life. None of the answers came near the questions my broken heart kept asking.

In *Too Soon Old, Too Late Smart*, author Gordon Livingston describes how during training maneuvers in Georgia, he was confused and anxious when the land surrounding him did not match the map he had in his hands. A wise army instructor said to him: "When the map and the ground do not agree, the map is wrong."

The same is true with our life maps. Life maps are gifts from people who have loved us most and wanted us not to get lost along the way: parents, teachers, mentors, ministers, heroes of all sorts. Those life maps we carry through the years provide dependable direction and guidance most of the time. The crisis occurs when the map no longer describes the terrain and is at odds with questions that will not go away. For years such maps define the path that reminds us of what we value and even who we are, until that moment when the map and ground no longer agree.

It is said that as Gertrude Stein lay dying, her life-long companion Alice Toklas, bending over her, whispered, "Gertrude, Gertrude, what is the answer?"

"Alice," Gertrude said to her, "Alice, what is the question?"

It is when the old answers no longer work that new questions defy trusted life maps.

If the ground and the map do not agree, we want to believe it is the ground that is wrong. When new questions surface in a relationship or career, in raising children or managing an office, when hopes get broken and uncharted disappointments, failures, and crises happen, we tenaciously hold on to old maps that tell us how to maneuver the unexpected and unknown. When hard times come, the last thing most of us want is a new map.

Families, churches, and even nations have maps that got them through tough times in the past, and so they depend on them for the future. In his book *Collapse*, Jared Diamond, professor of geography at the University of California, Los Angeles, describes how a thousand years ago the Norse of Greenland perished because they were intent on being Norwegians in a new land that could not sustain their traditional way of life. Archeologists have found only a few fish bones as evidence that the Norse chose to raise cattle and eat meat as they had done for centuries in Norway rather than imitate their Inuit neighbors and live off the bounty of the surrounding sea.

Why did the Norse choose not to eat fish? Because their life map said nothing about biological survival and everything about their cultural survival. Food taboos define family or community maps. Not eating fish served the same function for the Norse as building lavish churches and doggedly replicating the untenable agricultural practices of their land of origin. It was part of what it meant to be Norse. If you are going to establish a community in a harsh and forbidding environment, all those idiosyncrasies that define and cement a culture are of paramount importance. Having crossed the frontier and entered a strange land, they were intent on using the same map.

"The Norse were undone by the same social glue that had enabled them to master Greenland's difficulties," Jared Diamond writes. "The values to which people cling most stubbornly under inappropriate conditions are those values that were previously the source of their greatest triumphs over adversity. To us in our secular modern society, the predicament in which the Greenlanders found themselves is difficult to fathom. To them, however, concerned with their social survival as much as their biological survival, it was out of the question to invest less in churches, to imitate or intermarry with the Inuit, and thereby to face an eternity in Hell just in order to survive another winter on Earth."[68]

What do you know of such a map, one that charts the values, destiny, purpose—and even the gods—of your nation, your community, your church, your business, your profession, or your family? Where did your personal life map come from? Who crafted the terrain and marked the path? Who taught you your strategy for negotiating the geography, landscape, and wilderness? What do you know of trying times and tough choices, when your map has worked and gotten you through safely? What about occasions when it has confined you and held you hostage?

Boundaries and borders of our life maps can become barricades and barriers to speaking words of pain and sadness—and censors for expressions of intimacy to those we love. They define hope and keep a tight rein on expectations of who we are and who we might become. Inherited maps of our inner geography have boundaries and borders that determine what we permit ourselves to wonder about, question, feel, and desire deeply. Life maps are not just about the way we see the world, but also about the way we perceive and even define ourselves. Indeed, our maps even define God and show us what being religious—or choosing not to be religious—means to us.

Wanderings and Wonderings

Jesus leaves his Jewish homeland in Galilee and goes to the border of the Gentile territory of Tyre and Sidon. Could it be because something has wooed, tempted, or even called him? If so, what? Moreover, in leaving Galilee, who or what might Jesus want to leave behind or discover in another place?

Imagine neighbors or strangers see her as she comes out and shouts at him for mercy. What might they be thinking or saying? A non-Jewish mother pleads before this Galilean Jew for her daughter. The same Greek word is translated here as "left that place" and "came out." Matthew thus puts us on notice that he is telling a story in which both Jesus and a Canaanite woman, whose tribes are ancient enemies, "come out." Jesus coming out of his familiar home turf and the woman presumably coming out of her house in a foreign land set the stage. But what did they come out of? And what have they come into?

Read the story over several times. Then standing up, close your eyes and be the story. Be the woman. In your mind's eye see Jesus drawing near. Take a step and come out toward him. Shout, "Have mercy on me, Lord, Son of David; my daughter is tormented by a demon." You wait for a response. Silence. No answer at all. You hear his disciples urging him to send you away, and you hear his response to them. You take a step closer and kneel before him. "Lord, help me." He speaks to you, saying it is not fair to throw the children's food to the dogs. You agree, "Yes, Lord, yet even the dogs eat the crumbs that fall from their masters' table." He then says to you, "Woman, great is your faith! Let it be done for you as you wish." Take time to be still before you stand.

Pause. Take a deep breath, again close your eyes, and this time be one of the disciples. You are nearby when the woman begins shouting. You speak out to Jesus, "Send her away, for she keeps shouting after us." He answers in words you have heard before. He answers in words you already know are about him as well as about you: "I was sent only to the lost sheep of the house of Israel." Watching, you see her approach and kneel before Jesus. You listen. You hear him speak of her great faith, telling her that what she wishes will be done. Ponder what is happening for you.

After another deep breath, close your eyes and be Jesus. Leave "that place" called Galilee, the only world you know. Step over the line and cross the boundary into a strange and unknown land. You hear the woman shouting at you, asking for mercy. You do not answer her a word. The disciples come and urge you to send her away. You remind them, "I was sent only to the lost sheep of the house of Israel." The woman draws closer to you. Kneeling before you, she asks you to help her. You respond, "It is not fair to take the children's food and throw it to the dogs." You hear your own words as she agrees with you, yet she persists. "Then Jesus answered her." You answer her. Only then, after an awful silence and the devastating "No," do you now say to her, "Woman, great is your faith! Let it be done for you as you wish." Feel what it might be like to be in Jesus' shoes.

Write down from the inside out what it was like for you to experience being the woman, one of the disciples, and Jesus. Include any additional perceptions, questions, or confusion concerning each character and the connections between them.

- To what is Jesus initially saying yes?
  - And then no?
- What is the yes that the woman will not relinquish or surrender?
  - And the no she is unwilling to accept as an answer?
  - What brings her to that place of believing she has nothing to lose, allowing her to gamble everything on her no rather than submitting or agreeing or walking silently away?
- How would you describe to someone what is going on between Jesus and the woman?
  - Between Jesus and the disciples?
  - Inside the woman, the disciples, and Jesus?

Jesus speaks of the Canaanite woman's great faith. In your own words, describe her great faith. Discover for yourself what she is doing or saying that leads her to the healing she seeks.

- What do you discover here, in this story, about Jesus' life map? And those maps within the disciples—and even the woman?

As the story ends, think of new questions that may now haunt, preoccupy, mystify, and challenge the woman, the disciples, and Jesus. See Jesus leaving the place, going up the mountain beside the sea, and sitting down alone. Imagine his feelings and thoughts and what he may wonder and pray about.

Look around. Today, two thousand years later, people and institutions are also being called to risk crossing frontiers into unfamiliar and challenging places that might teach them about their past, present, and future.

- Who are they and where are they?
- How do you see them being invited to read the life maps they use to make sense of the world with new eyes?

And you. Name and label the outsider—the marginal and even alien inner Canaanite woman—who keeps you restless and disturbed by your life and the world. Listen to the enemy voices: job loss, cancer, divorce, old age, violence, high oil prices, pornography, pollution, global warming, terrorism, and AIDS.

- Where, when, and how do these voices plead with you to reassess things you are certain about and take for granted?
- What do you know of a voice from within calling you to question what seems always to have been true?
- What might you gain and what might you have to give up if your no turns into a yes?
- Under what circumstances, pressures, threats, hopes, yearnings, or dreams do you refuse to take no as an answer?

Imagine what the teller of this story may well want you to know about the life map that you rely on to chart your life. Then return to life maps you have in your drawers, pockets, psyche, and soul, and remember when they gave you good direction and when you discovered they didn't agree with the ground. Remember also the frontiers you've crossed and those you've looked at from a distance because your map said, "Don't go there." Journal about how you know this story as your story. Include the places in your real and in your imaginary landscapes where you encounter all the characters, including the tormented daughter. Revisit those journeys, but also look beyond your doorway or window at the road you never take— and even at the horizon—and wonder.

To cross a frontier is to be transformed. The frontier is a wake-up call. At the frontier we can't avoid the truth; the comforting layers of the quotidian, which insulate us against the world's harsher realities, are stripped away and, wide-eyed in the harsh fluorescent light of the frontier's windowless halls, we see things as they are.
> —Salman Rushdie, *Step Across the Line: Collected Nonfiction 1992–2002*[69]

To regret one's own experience is to arrest one's own development. To deny one's own experience is to put a lie into the lips of one's own life. It is no less than a denial of the soul.
> —Oscar Wilde, *The Portable Oscar Wilde*[70]

If we really want to communicate, we have to give up knowing what to do. When we come in with our agendas, they only block us from seeing the person in front of us. It's best to drop our five-year plans and accept the awkward sinking feelings that we are entering a situation naked. We don't know what will happen next or what we'll do.
> —Pema Chodrön, *Start Where You Are: A Guide to Compassionate Living*[71]

"And remember, also," added the Princess of Sweet Rhyme, "that many places you would like to see are just off the map and many things you want to know are just out of sight or a little beyond your reach. But someday you'll reach them all, for what you learn today, for no reason at all, will help you discover all the wonderful secrets of tomorrow."
> —Norton Juster, *The Phantom Tollbooth*[72]

The Opening of Eyes
by David Whyte[73]

> That day I saw beneath dark clouds
> the passing light over the water
> and I heard the voice of the world speak out,
> I knew then, as I had before,
> life is no passing memory of what has been
> nor the remaining pages in a great book
> waiting to be read.

It is the opening of eyes long closed.
It is the vision of far-off things
seen for the silence they hold.
It is the heart after years
of secret conversing
speaking out loud in the clear air.

It is Moses in the desert
fallen to his knees before the lit bush.
It is the man throwing away his shoes
as if to enter heaven
and finding himself astonished,
opened at last,
fallen in love with solid ground.

Parable of the Fictionist
by Stephen Dunn[74]

He wanted to own his own past,
be able to manage it
more than it managed him.
He wanted all the unfair
advantages of the charmed.
He selected his childhood,
told only those stories
that mixed loneliness with
rebellion, a boy's locked heart
with the wildness
allowed inside a playing field.
And after he invented himself
and those he wished to know him
knew him as he wished to be known,
he turned toward the world
with the world that was within him
and shapes resulted, versions,
enlargements.
In his leisure he invented women,
then spoke to them about
his inventions, the wish just
slightly ahead of the truth,
making it possible.

All around him he heard
the unforgivable stories
of the sincere, the boring,
and knew his way was righteous,
though in the evenings, alone
with the world he's created,
he sometimes longed
for what he'd dare not alter,
or couldn't, something immutable
or so lovely he might be changed
by it, nameless but with a name
he feared waits until you're worthy,
then chooses you.

In View of the Fact
by A. R. Ammons[75]

The people of my time are passing away: my
wife is baking for a funeral, a 60-year-old who

died suddenly, when the phone rings, and it's
Ruth we care so much about in intensive care:

it was once weddings that came so thick and
fast, and then, first babies, such a hullabaloo:

now, it's this that and the other and somebody
else gone or on the brink: well, we never

thought we would live forever (although we did)
and now it looks like we won't: some of us

are losing a leg to diabetes, some don't know
what they went downstairs for, some know that

a hired watchful person is around, some like
to touch the cane tip into something steady,

so nice: we have already lost so many,
brushed the loss of ourselves ourselves: our

address books for so long a slow scramble now
are palimpsests, scribbles and scratches: our

index cards for Christmases, birthdays,
Halloweens drop clean away into sympathies:

at the same time we are getting used to so
many leaving, we are hanging on with a grip

to the ones left: we are not giving up on the
congestive heart failure or brain tumors, on

the nice old men left in empty houses or on
the widows who decide to travel a lot: we

think the sun may shine someday when we'll
drink wine together and think of what used to

be: until we die we will remember every
single thing, recall every word, love every

loss: then we will, as we must, leave it to
others to love, love that can grow brighter

and deeper till the very end, gaining strength
and getting more precious all the way. . . .

ELEVEN

CHOOSING LIFE

They came to Jericho. As he and his disciples and a large crowd were leaving Jericho, Bartimaeus son of Timaeus, a blind beggar, was sitting by the roadside. When he heard that it was Jesus of Nazareth, he began to shout out and say, "Jesus, Son of David, have mercy on me!" Many sternly ordered him to be quiet, but he cried out even more loudly, "Son of David, have mercy on me!" Jesus stood still and said, "Call him here."

And they called the blind man, saying to him, "Take heart; get up, he is calling you." So throwing off his cloak, he sprang up and came to Jesus. Then Jesus said to him, "What do you want me to do for you?" The blind man said to him, "My teacher, let me see again." Jesus said to him, "Go, your faith has made you well." Immediately he regained his sight and followed him on the way. (Mark 10:46–52)

Reflections
BY BILL

My very first visit to Boston in 1967 began before dawn at an airport in Wilmington, North Carolina. The early-morning flight included four intermediate stops. On this particular day, full flights and bad weather caused schedules to go awry, and by the time I got to National Airport in Washington, DC, connections to Boston were few. So it was not until late afternoon that I finally landed at Logan Airport and set out to drive to nearby Cambridge.

Many things may have changed in Boston since that time, including the Big Dig tunnel beneath the city, but the traffic and congestion coming out of the airport are still the same. In a rental car with the map that marked my way sitting in my lap, I drove out of the airport into at least six lanes of bumper-to-bumper rush-hour traffic as I searched for the Starrow Drive exit. Driving for my life, it was too late to turn off as my exit veered off to the right without me. All I knew to do was punt. As best I could, I edged into the next exit lane and only recall glancing up to see a sign for the USS *Constitution* as I headed off the highway down the ramp. Reaching the bottom, I figured there would be a gas station where I could get help. Wrong. It was also clear this was no place for a preacher from North Carolina to be getting lost.

I drove a few blocks before pulling into a "gas station"—a tiny shack sitting behind the two pumps. No one came out. I went in. I can still see the man in charge sitting with his feet up on his makeshift desk. I figured it was time to go for broke. Standing before his desk I took a very deep breath and said as calmly as I could, "Mister, I really need your help. I'm in trouble. I left Wilmington, North Carolina, early this morning in the dark, and I have been to Jacksonville, Kinston, Greenville, Norfolk, and then Washington, where I missed my plane and the weather turned bad, and I have never been to Boston. . . ." Bored with my litany, the man waved his hand to stop me and said, "Mister, I don't care where you have been. I just want to know where the hell do you want to go!"

In his poem "The Opening of Eyes," David Whyte writes, "I knew then, as I had before, life is no passing memory of what has been nor the remaining pages in a great book waiting to be read."[76] As the man in the gas station had pointed out to me, the question is not about where you have been but about where you want to go. It is not about rehearsing and repeating that endless mantra of should haves and should not haves, nor is it about all those fantasy projections of what is yet to be. Rather it is about where you want to go and what you want to have happen in your life now. Right now. Not redoing the past. Not predicting the future. Today.

Weight Watchers has made a subtle but significant tweak to their sales pitch for a lean body. In recent television ads the slim young woman on the beach tells us that the only question she was asked when she went to Weight Watchers was what she wanted to be in her life. No talk about pounds to lose or diets to keep. Everything is now focused on who you want to be and what kind of life you want to live. Everything else flows from your answer to that one point-blank question.

I recall as a very young father sitting at the dining room table with my five-year-old daughter, Jennifer, to my right. She begins doing something that greatly displeases me—something unforgivable like putting her elbows on the table or talking with food in her mouth. So I stare hard and in silence at her, imitating my father's way to discipline me at such moments. Then I see tears well up in her little eyes that look toward me with apprehension mixed with love. I know, years later, what being looked at like that did for me and the kind of relationship it created with my father. Do I want the same thing for the two of us? Is that what I really want?

So what do you want? Finding the answer requires what Whyte explores when writing of "the opening of eyes long closed. It is the vision of far-off things seen for the silence they hold."[77] For most of us some of the time, and for a few of us all the time, life is keeping eyes closed to what is going on around the kitchen table or conference table or desk or altar. It is a way of never having to wonder about the amazing and terrifying possibilities that wait to happen in our lives. Opening eyes to look into the eyes of others—and into the mirror—carries the promise and the risk of the heart speaking out loud in the clear air after years of secret conversing.

Poet Kenneth Fearing describes a young woman sitting with her husband in the family room after a long and wearisome day. They lose themselves in the blur of television light. They have talked a little, but not enough, and have tried to make the time pass with a drink, until the eleven o'clock news is over, and she says she thinks she will go up. "Are you coming soon?" she asks. And he says, "In a minute," but as she heads toward the stairs, she hears him switch to a late show, and she knows that he'll spend another hour watching TV and she'll drift off to sleep alone—again. As she climbs the stairs in the dark, she does that silly thing she used to do as a child when she was afraid and counts the steps, and in the darkness, not wanting to and wishing she hadn't, she asks herself, did I sometime or somewhere have a different idea? Pausing to decide whether to go upstairs alone or to go back downstairs alone, she wonders for the first time in her life, is this what I was born to feel and to do and to be?

Seeing the world and ourselves in a new way does not happen by turning over a new leaf, making more promises and resolutions, changing our behavior, or even going on a diet. When Jesus meets blind Bartimaeus in the streets of Jericho, he does not give him a list of commandments or a set of rules or a map of shoulds and oughts. He begins by asking him a question: *What do you want?* Until you know what you want and who you want to be, no weight loss scheme or spiritual exercise or big bank account or university degree is going to make any difference. It begins by asking a question: *What do I want?*

Wanderings and Wonderings

Imagine yourself to be the blind beggar named Bartimaeus sitting by the roadside in the town of Jericho. Sit on the floor with your eyes closed and become Bartimaeus. Be immersed in the sounds and smells that surround you. Hear the noise and the voices. Beg for alms. Give words to the darkness that is your world day after day. Consider your place in the world, the way you get along with all the others—those who stop and those who pass you by. Ponder your future and what it holds.

A crowd comes by. When you hear that Jesus is among them, you shout out to him, "Jesus, Son of David, have mercy on me!" Describe the mercy for which you cry. Mutter the words of rebuke directed at you. Give yourself reasons why they are so stern as they order you, a blind beggar, to be silent.

You cry out all the more. Jesus stops and stands still. He tells his companions to call you over to him. Springing up, you throw off the cloak that defines you to all the world as a beggar.

Jesus asks, "What do you want me to do for you?" Wonder about such a question when the answer seems so obvious.

- Is there something else that you, a blind beggar, want other than your sight?
- Why might Jesus ask you that question?
- What does this question do to and for you?

Jesus tells you to go, for "your faith has made you well."

- Jesus says nothing about having healed you. He attributes your seeing to "your faith." How—in what you have done and said—have you exhibited a "faith" in something or someone other than Jesus?
- Describe the tension between Jesus, you, and those who sternly order you to be quiet.

Recall a time recently when you sensed that you could no longer see, or that you lacked vision, or that you were blind to what was going on within and around you. Ask yourself:

- What do I spend my days watching in order to avoid seeing?
- How are my words and actions cries for mercy? What kind of mercy do I long for?
- How am I shouting out for more from life in the way I eat, drink, play, work, love?

Listen to the voices rebuking the Bartimaeus within you, ordering you to be silent.

- How do those voices—the ones within you and the ones without— devour the longing and swallow up the hope of what you want, of what you yearn for?

In your personal drama, what brings your inner Jesus to a standstill, compelling him to ignore all your internal voices that try to silence the blind beggar within you? What is it that urges this Jesus to call out to the Bartimaeus in your heart? And what is the cloak—the camouflage or disguise you wear—that, like Bartimaeus, you must throw off in the hope of healing? Are you willing to take the risk of letting that cloak go?

Again hear the question Jesus asks—what do you want?—and write down something of the healing and wholeness for which you yearn in your most significant relationships, your family, your job, studies, health, heart, guilty conscience, or sagging spirit.

- If you were healed from whatever blindness or infirmity keeps a part of your body or spirit in darkness, how might your life be different?
- Along with the new hopes and joys, what fears and unforeseen demands might arise?

A blind beggar named Bartimaeus sits by the roadside until Jesus asks him what he wants done for him. When Bartimaeus replies, Jesus says, "Go, your faith has made you well."

Deep within you, what do you know of a "faith" named Bartimaeus that is longing to shout, waiting to happen, and ready to throw off a mantle and lead you to healing and wholeness?

Mirrors

Boys, you must strive to find your own voice. Because the longer you wait to begin, the less likely you are to find it at all. Thoreau said, "Most men lead lives of quiet desperation." Don't be resigned to that. Break out!
—John Keating, in the film *Dead Poets Society*[78]

Once in Chicago at the Hilton I slipped
an "I quit" note under my boss' door.

Whatever I love about my life
started there.
　　—Stephen Dunn, "Loves," in *New and Selected Poems
　　　1974–1994*[79]

When I awake in the morning,
It is either the very next day
after many, many days
Or it is the very first day.
Today, it is the very first day
Of what exists now.
　　—Twainhart Hill, from *Ode to My Father*[80]

In the western tradition, we were taught many things about the nature of
sin, but we were never told that one of the greatest sins is the unlived life.
　　—John O'Donohue, *Anam Cara: A Book of Celtic Wisdom*[81]

For a long time it had seemed to me that life was about to begin, real life.
But there was always some obstacle in the way, something to be gotten
through first, some unfinished business, time still to be served, a debt to
be paid. Then life would begin. At last it dawned on me that these obstacles were my life.
　　—Alfred D'Souza[82]

From *Holy Hunger: A Woman's Journey from Food Addiction to Spiritual Fulfillment* by Margaret Bullitt-Jonas[83]

Here is the story I would like to tell about my life: The story of a woman
growing up confused about her desires, uncertain whether it was even
acceptable to have desires, uncertain about what to do with the ones she
had. A woman persistently looking outside herself for what she was hungry
for. A woman growing up in a culture that was all too ready to tell her what
she wanted and to create a climate of craving. A card-carrying member of a
culture that urges all of us to eat, shop, buy, acquire; for there in the material
good around us, in possessions and commodities, prizes and grades, accom-
plishments and lovers, doughnuts and ice cream, surely we'll find what we're
looking for, our heart's desire. The story of a woman who was perpetually
restless, afraid of her own emptiness, afraid to listen to her longing . . .

　　I tried to quell my desires. Eradicate them. Transcend them . . . My infinite longing devolved into insatiable craving . . . I couldn't speak my story,

could find neither words nor silence that helped me connect. So I choked off my words. Filled up the silence . . . At last . . . [at] a crossroad . . . I had to choose between life and death. As starkly as that. And it was life that I chose, life that chose me. A day at a time . . . I learned to stop killing myself . . .

From *A Home at the End of the World*
by Michael Cunningham[84]

"This is going to be hard, hard for me to say. But I've been thinking. Do you ever, well, wonder about us? I mean, about you and me?"

"I think about us," Jonathan says. "Sure I do."

"I don't mean just *think*. I don't mean just that, I mean, well, do you ever wonder why we always held back? It seems like we could have done so much more to make each other happy."

"Well, we had a certain kind of relationship," Jonathan responds. "It was pretty much what we both wanted, wasn't it?"

"I guess so. I guess it was," says Erich. "But lately I've been wondering, you know. I've been wondering, what were we waiting for?"

"I suppose we were waiting for our real lives to start. I think we probably made a mistake."

"We did make a mistake," Erich says to him. "I mean, I think we probably did. I think I was in love with you, and I couldn't admit it. I was, I don't know. Too afraid to admit it. And now it just seems like a waste. We could have done better than this, you and I. What was the matter with us?"

"I don't know," Jonathan says.

Neither moves or speaks for at least a minute. They stare at each other in furious disbelief.

"We're cowards," he adds to the list. "This wasn't a dramatic mistake we made. It was just a stupid little one that got out of hand. What do they call them? Sins of omission."

Erich: "I think that's what bothers me most."

Jonathan: "Me, too."

From "Theme from Mahogany"
by Michael Masser and Gerry Goffin

> Do you know where you're going to?
> Do you like the things that life is showing you?
> Where are you going to, do you know?
> Do you get what you're hoping for?
> When you look behind you there's no open door,
> What are you hoping for, do you know?

TWELVE

DISCOVERING GOD'S KINGDOM

He also said, "With what can we compare the kingdom of God, or what parable will we use for it? It is like a mustard seed, which, when sown upon the ground, is the smallest of all the seeds on earth; yet when it is sown it grows up and becomes the greatest of all shrubs, and puts forth large branches, so that the birds of the air can make nests in its shade. (Mark 4:30–32)

Reflections
BY CAREN

Back in the early 1950s—before air conditioners became standard household stock—Jewish families fled to enclaves in the mountains to escape the stifling summer heat radiating off the sidewalks of New York. Most headed for the infamous land of Jewish jokes: the Catskills. However, others chose lesser-known routes and settled into Jewish resorts in nearby states.

In 1954, after rejecting the idea of spending the upcoming summer at a hotel or leasing a bungalow in a "colony," my parents decided to stake a more permanent claim on one of God's little acres. After just a quick visit to Mt. Freedom, New Jersey, they bought a two-bedroom, nine-hundred-square-foot white clapboard house on one acre. In fact, it was not just in the resort town but stood on the highest point of the eponymous mountain.

Despite dual realities that their property sprouted mostly pernicious weeds instead of grass and that the tiny homestead needed extensive repairs, my parents called it their Promised Land. And so the last day of school that year, after packing my younger sister, the dog, and me into the back seat of the car, my parents began their first exodus to the mountain-top an hour west of the city. While driving out of Brooklyn, across the East River and under the Hudson, my father made clear his unshakable resolve to have a pristine lawn and a vegetable garden in his domain: "God will-ing." Unfortunately, within days of our arrival, it became obvious that the weeds' determination to hold on to their turf would be equally tenacious.

In his efforts to be lord and master, assert control, and ultimately pre-vail over the wicked weeds, my father demanded that my mother, sister, and I take immediate action. Our job, he commanded, was to purge the land of them. Pick, dig, yank, and destroy till they were no more. Further-more, we had to be especially mindful that those we pulled and packed into piles to be burned did not spill their seed or sprout volunteers in the newly planted tomatoes all around the house.

To strategize ways to purge the enemy, my father read late into the night and sought the counsel of more experienced weed-slayers. And while doing actual battle in the field, he probably set weed-pulling records while cursing his foes. But despite his contemplating, conversing, and damning, nothing defeated the onslaught of the wily weeds. Moreover, as his frus-tration with the land, his daily commute back and forth to the city, busi-ness problems, and family rifts escalated, my mother, sister, and I became targets of his anger. We were slacking off when he was working twelve hours daily to pay for the luxury of us being here and not there, he said. We didn't appreciate what was given us and took it for granted, he com-plained. "You're the real weeds. You!" he screamed at our horrified faces.

Given the right conditions, lots of weeds can grow on one acre or in one's heart. And with few exceptions, they have no respect for boundaries. Property lines, fences, and neat, differentiated gardens mean nothing to them. When my father saw that generations of weeds were also deeply rooted in the bordering woods, he ordered us to go forth and conquer them, too. We tried, vainly, for several days until the red spots and pus-tules popping up on our skin halted our efforts. The doctor named our condition poison ivy and reminded us it was a weed that didn't grow much in Brooklyn. The data offered little comfort in the days that followed as the poison ivy spread—beyond our arms and legs, onto our trunks, and into our mouths, noses, and ears. In response, we itched, and tried not to scratch, and doused ourselves with calamine, and cried. Being only seven, I began to hate our haven and prayed hard to God to either kill the weeds or lead us back to the city.

My prayers went unanswered, and so did my father's. By the end of sum-mer, the weeds had prevailed. As a perverse counterpoint the tomatoes did, too, despite being infested with weeds and worms. That's because my urban parents didn't know that you only need a couple of plants to feed a family of four, and so they planted two hundred. By mid-August, no matter where one walked, one kicked, stepped on, or slid on rotten red beefsteaks, cherries, and plums. Not surprisingly, every year afterwards leftover tomato seeds dispersed by wind, weather, and wildlife germinated everywhere.

The summer following our first one, my father planted four tomato, two pepper, and some cucumber plants in a well-defined patch. He also added six more acres of land to his kingdom, and his abiding fixation on weeds escalated. Predictably, my mother, sister, and I failed to live up to his expectation that we would or could clear seven acres.

During the summer of 1960, my parents decided to exit Brooklyn forever and live in Mt. Freedom year-round. For them the move offered the hope that they could begin anew during a particularly difficult time in their marriage. However, rather than temper my father's obsessions, the move fed them and they grew. To the established crops of dandelions, crabgrass, and other weeds around us, he gradually brought new ones into our lives: alcohol, gambling, and a twisted understanding of Judaism that became so invasive, unruly, oppressive, and demanding that my mother left his kingdom forever.

Before dying in 1994, my father continued to live as a recluse in the new house he built alongside the old shortly before his divorce. He called it "The Shondarosa," a Yiddish play on words that means "beautiful shame." Three decades earlier, I had left the mountaintop to go to college in the Midwest. Once out the door, I never again lived in New Jersey.

For a long time I stayed away from Mt. Freedom. But as I began identifying what belonged and didn't belong in my life and in the gardens I was planting, tending, pruning, and perpetuating, I became determined to see my father's world from new perspectives. In stages, I began visiting—first alone and then with my growing family—to help me get at the roots of what I was planting for future generations and maybe even understand what my father's efforts to destroy the weeds in his kingdom were really all about.

While living his own questions about the purpose of weeds, essayist Ralph Waldo Emerson concluded that they were plants "whose virtues have not yet been discovered." In the years after my father died, I revisited my memories of the real and imagined weeds that took over his life, and I struggled to understand where undiscovered virtues could be found. Finally, one day as I was warning my young granddaughter not to touch a poison ivy plant, a forgotten episode unfolded.

Whoever built our summer home on top of Mt. Freedom planted it in the middle of an abandoned asparagus farm. On the first day of our second summer, after a long winter spent contemplating weeds, my father said, "Aha," donned gloves, walked into the thick poison ivy in the woods, and picked the asparagus crop that still sprung up. He cooked the tender plants, turned a deaf ear to my mother's protests that we'd get sick, and made us eat from plates heaped with thin, green, undercooked stalks. I never got poison ivy that summer long ago—not even when I stood in the midst of it in my failed attempts to weed the rest of the woods. In fact, I never got it again.

Wanderings and Wonderings

Before you begin to explore the overarching question posited by the parable, consider the following.

No matter what your faith or spiritual roots, it is possible that you have already heard this parable, a variation on the theme, and even explanations of its meaning. Perhaps in a book of Bible stories, perhaps in a sermon or article, or perhaps because you saw someone wearing a mustard seed on a chain and asked why. If you can, imagine that you are a first-century Jew who has come to hear these words of Jesus for the first time.

This parable is about a specific seed. Look at the information the text in Mark's gospel gives you about a mustard seed. See what words describing this particular seed stand out for you, and then allow your mind to wander beyond the passage and think literally and metaphorically about seeds overall. Take into account what they look like, what their function is, what they contain before opening, and what must happen if they are to germinate and become something else.

Although most people eat and enjoy mustard, few know that the plant that grows from a mustard seed germinates quickly. Depending on the variety of mustard, the plant develops into a weedy shrub that is anywhere from two to six feet tall. Even domestic varieties get out of control and often become a nuisance. In Mark's gospel, it is most likely that the plant referred to is Black Mustard (*Brassica nigra*), the tallest of the Middle Eastern mustard plants. It could grow to six feet.

In Jesus' time people used mustard for multiple reasons. Indeed, the Roman author Pliny the Elder, who died in 79 CE when scientific curiosity brought him too close to an erupting Vesuvius, wrote:

Pythagoras judged it [mustard] to be the chief of those plants whose pungent properties reach a high level, since no other penetrates further into the nostrils and brain. Pounded, it is applied with vinegar to the bites of serpents and scorpion stings. It counteracts the poisons of fungi. For phelgm it is kept in the mouth until it melts, or is used as a gargle with hydromel (a mixture of water and honey that becomes mead when fermented).

For toothache it is chewed. . . . It is very beneficial for all stomach troubles. . . . It clears the senses, and by the sneezing caused by it, the head; it relaxes the bowels, it promotes menstruation and urine.

However, Pliny also wrote:

It grows entirely wild, though it is improved by being transplanted: but on the other hand when it has once been sown it is scarcely possible to get the place free of it, as the seed, when it falls, germinates at once.[85]

Furthermore, in Jesus' time one was not supposed to sow mustard seed in a garden because plants couldn't be mixed ("You shall not sow your field with two kinds of seed"—Leviticus 19:19; and "You shall not sow your vineyard with a second kind of seed, or the whole yield will have to be forfeited, both the crop that you have sown and the yield of the vineyard itself"—Deuteronomy 22:9). Each variety needed its own space. Since mustard is a seed-bearing plant and volunteers can shoot up anywhere and everywhere, mustard could be cultivated in a field, but it was considered unclean in a garden.

Say aloud Jesus' opening words that ask what the kingdom of God can be compared to. *Empire* is another word for kingdom. In the first century, Jesus' audiences would hear references not only to the kingdom of God, but to the empire of God and kingdom of heaven also. The former was used in opposition to the empire of Caesar, a phrase used by the occupying and oppressive Roman armies and rule. So when Jesus' audience used or heard the phrase "empire of God," it was intended to be a counterpoint to the autocratic rule over them by the tight and orderly Roman oppressors whom Caesar carefully and strategically planted in Jerusalem.

With all that in mind, imagine you are a loyalist to the empire of Caesar, standing on the fringes of a crowd listening to Jesus compare the kingdom of God to a mustard seed. You know something about mustard seeds and mustard plants. You also know that for Jesus' Jewish audience the empire of Caesar is the enemy.

- What do you hear Jesus saying about the potential held in that seed?
- If allowed to germinate, what might this kingdom of God be or represent or do within the boundaries of the well-ordered empire of Caesar?

Now, using whatever art materials you have on hand, create a picture of a perfect garden—your perfect garden. You could also create one by making a collage or taking a picture with a digital camera. Then sit with your perfect garden and recall who taught you how to plant and maintain gardens.

When you feel ready, add weeds—ones from your garden or ones penciled or crayoned in—to your picture.

Place the picture in front of you and again sit with it. Recall an actual experience of having unwanted, prolific, noxious, invasive, unwelcome, offensive, and aggressive weeds of any kind in your flowerbed, yard, or vegetable patch, or in a community garden, a nearby vacant lot, or the yard of an abandoned house.

- Who taught you to call those plants weeds?
- And when you saw them in your flowerbed, yard, vegetable patch, or other places nearby, how did you react and/or feel about having to deal with them?

Look around and see where and how you have planted well-tended, orderly gardens in your life. Not just the ones outside your front or back door, but those in other places and in your psyche and soul, too.

- Symbolically, who or what are unwanted, prolific, noxious, invasive, unwelcome, offensive, and aggressive "weeds" that break through their protective shells and germinate, taking root in the world around those gardens?
- And what about the weeds in the world that cross boundaries and thresholds and make their way into your carefully tended, orderly personal gardens?
- Are those "weeds" people, conditions, situations, thoughts, feelings, obsessions, or desires—or something else?
- What might weeds in your life be trying to alert you to in the world and in your life?
- And what might those weeds be trying to tell you about the kingdom of God?
- In your journal, finish the sentence, "The kingdom of God is like . . ."

Additionally, reflect on your ongoing efforts to maintain order and weed the established and tidy garden that is your life. Now re-read your sentence describing the kingdom of God and ask yourself, why am I doing that?

Man becomes aware of the Sacred because it manifests itself, shows itself, as something wholly different from the Profane. . . . In his encounters with the Sacred, man experiences a reality that does not belong to our world yet is encountered in and through objects or events that are part of the world.

>—Mircea Eliade, *The Sacred and Profane: The Nature of Religion*[86]

The more we understand individual things, the more we understand God.

>—Benedict De Spinoza, from *The Gift of Truth: Gathering the Good* by Stephen Ross[87]

As with all new science, genetic manipulation of seed DNA has possibilities for good and for evil. It depends on how it's used and who controls it.

>—Ruth S. Foster, from "Seeds" by Michael Garofalo[88]

What would become of the garden if the gardener treated all the weeds and slugs and birds and trespassers as he would like to be treated, if he were in their place?

>—Thomas Henry Huxley, *Evolution and Ethics*[89]

Purple Loosestrife
by Ann Townsend[90]

>Purple loosestrife
>is too good to be true, in all its definitions.
>Once beloved, once beautiful: today the wildflower magazines
>apologize for including it. It induces wrath
>in water-gardeners everywhere. Crews of volunteers
>uproot and burn the plants from marshes in Minnesota.

>Like the remedies of revisionists, it does the job
>too well—like kudzu or hybrid trout, anything introduced
>with good intentions. It wipes out the competition.
>Where it grows best it is least desired.
>You can't buy it in any nursery.

Doing its enterprising best it seeds itself,
driving out local weedy growth, what fits, what came first.
Best-named of all wild things, for those who love the names,
it casts itself into the swamps and will not quit.
Like an imperialist, it has changed the landscape forever.

From *Evensong*
by Gail Godwin[91]

"Where is God in all this?" I once typed angrily to him from seminary,
after a week on the third-floor ward at St. Luke's Hospital when I was
doing my Clinical Pastoral Education. "Twenty-five beds filled with rape,
shooting, and dope victims, and here's this young woman of eighteen, born
to be beautiful, with oozing, fresh razor scars all over her face *and* sickle
cell anemia, and the nurse in charge is withholding her morphine simply
because she's a sadist exercising her power. I was able to intervene about
the morphine, but I never could look directly at this young woman's
slashed-up beauty without fighting down the urge to run out of that ward
and forsake my presumptuous dreams of improving the world."
    He wrote back, by return mail that time:

> Your question may be the only one that matters. Despite all the convoluted
> guesswork of theologians ever since Job's friends hunched beside him on
> the dung heap, "Where is God in this?" (just the question itself alone, I
> mean) may be enough to keep us busy down here. Maybe the thing we're
> required to do is simply keep asking the question, as Job did—asking it faith-
> fully over and over, whatever ghastly thing is happening around us at the
> time—until God begins to reveal himself through the ways we are changed
> by the answering silence.

Long Live the Weeds
by Theodore Roethke[92]

Long live the weeds that overwhelm
My narrow vegetable realm! —
The bitter rock, the barren soil
That force the son of man to toil;
All things unholy, marked by curse,
The ugly of the universe.
The rough, the wicked, and the wild
That keep the spirit undefiled.

With these I match my little wit
And earn the right to stand or sit,
Hope, look, create, or drink or die:
These shape the creature that is I.

Bits of Rubble Turn into Gold
by Tz'u-min[93]

The Buddha, the causal stage, made the universal vow:
When beings hear my Name and think on me,
I will come to welcome each of them,
Not discriminating at all between the poor and the rich and
   well-born,
Not discriminating between the inferior and highly gifted,
Not choosing the learned and those upholding pure precepts,
Nor rejecting those who break precepts and whose evil karma
   is profound.
Solely making beings turn about and abundantly say the *nembutsu*,
I can make bits of rubble change into gold!

CHAPTER 13

ENTERING THE HEART
OF THE MATTER

When they had come near Jerusalem and had reached Bethphage, at the Mount of Olives, Jesus sent two disciples, saying to them, "Go into the village ahead of you, and immediately you will find a donkey tied, and a colt with her; untie them and bring them to me. If anyone says anything to you, just say this, 'The Lord needs them.' And he will send them immediately." This took place to fulfill what had been spoken through the prophet, saying,

"Tell the daughter of Zion, Look, your king is coming to you, humble, and mounted on a donkey, and on a colt, the foal of a donkey."

The disciples went and did as Jesus had directed them; they brought the donkey and the colt, and put their cloaks on them, and he sat on them. A very large crowd spread their cloaks on the road, and others cut branches from the trees and spread them on the road. The crowds that went ahead of him and that followed were shouting, "Hosanna to the Son of David! Blessed is the one who comes in the name of the Lord! Hosanna in the highest heaven!"

When he entered Jerusalem, the whole city was in turmoil, asking, "Who is this?" The crowds were saying, "This is the prophet Jesus from Nazareth in Galilee." Then Jesus entered the temple and drove out all who were selling and buying in the temple, and he overturned the tables of the money changers and the seats of those who sold doves. He said to them, "It is written, 'My house shall be called a house of prayer'; but you are making it a den of robbers." (Matthew 21:1–13)

Reflections

BY BILL

David and his wife live in a large and comfortable retirement home in the suburbs, where they enjoy security and some serenity in their early eighties. David has a friend he met when he first moved there seven years ago. Paul has since been widowed and, having suffered several strokes, now lives in an assisted care unit called Oasis Gardens. Several times a week David visits Paul, who, though the same age, now leans forward against the straps across his chest that attach him to the wheelchair. Parkinson's makes talking difficult. He tends to drool.

Every visit between David and Paul begins the same way. When David asks "How's it going?" Paul's confusing response is always: "You know how it is?" Like others, David finds it hard to know whether his friend is asking him a question or telling him an answer. So he nods knowingly and then they talk about everything in the world except what is going on right before them. David, who was ordained a minister fifty-some years ago, confesses that if he were visiting a parishioner, he would feel confident and know exactly what to say. Something comforting, religious, even a prayer would be a gentle and caring response, softening things. But for some mysterious reason this doesn't happen. It doesn't work that way. David doesn't know what to say. It has something to do, he speculates, with how he can't say something religious, do his minister thing, leave, and get out. This is his world as well, and if he is going anyplace, it is most likely Oasis Gardens, too.

The moment of revelation for David comes to us all when we stop—or are stopped—long enough to look at what we see in the mirror and are speechless: when the role we play doesn't wash anymore, when the spiel that has gotten us through tougher jams than this doesn't work. There is only the silence in the presence of what threatens to overwhelm, bewilder, disturb, and maybe destroy us. No words. There is only an ache in the heart, a tear in the eye, and a certainty that there is no exit or hiding place.

We have all been there once or twice. It is that awkward moment at dinner when you sense the gulf between you and your teenage son, and it dawns on you that the time for building bridges has slipped away while you were too busy with work or golf or church. It comes in the night many long years into the marriage when your wife rolls on her side, turning her back to you, and you hear her breathing deeply, almost sighing, wide awake—maybe sad or maybe angry but surely wondering about what might have been. Then the urge to run another mile or drink a third martini or gulp a pill or buy a dozen roses or clean up the bathroom or go shopping or plan a big vacation simply because you are speechless: you can talk about anything but what's not going on between and inside you.

Moments like that, when the props don't work and familiar roles flop, can, however, be a promising realization that finally we are all broken-down actors. That realization offers a chance to face the brokenness and embrace all the might have beens and could have beens. Such moments are about a part of us dying and, if we are brave enough, can lead us beyond our pretensions and illusions toward new possibilities for ourselves and the world.

Southport, North Carolina, is what they call "landfall": the last place pilots on northeastern flights southbound over the ocean can see solid ground before reaching the point of no return. Once Southport is behind, there is no longer a safe place to land. Only one place to go. Jesus enters into a Jerusalem that is the heart of Roman power and authority as well as the temple sanctuary and the abode of the God of his people. Jesus sets his face toward Jerusalem and passes his point of no return in dealings with the profane and the sacred powers of his world.

The final act that follows is brief and violent and lasts only hours. It is one of dishonor, defeat, and failure for Jesus—so much so that, ever since, those few days have led believers and nonbelievers alike to dissect the meaning of "failure."

The story that ends in three days in a dark tomb proposes what countless people have experienced since the beginning of time: new life is born not so much through power and victory as through defeat and death. Healing happens in Rome and the temple, in relationships that matter most, and in the hungry heart only when we are broken and naked, left speechless without glib answers, without sufficient duct tape to put it all back together again. Healing happens in those terrible moments when we realize we are not going to be saved by the marines or rescued by Homeland Security; that no divine intercessor is going to deliver us from our fears or liberate us from our illness. Healing happens in the excruciating moments when we discover that being vulnerable and wounded is where healing is hidden, and where it waits as well for those who lean forward, saying, "You know how it is?"

Wanderings and Wonderings

Imagine being outside the city watching Jesus of Nazareth as he draws close to the walled and golden city of Jerusalem, sitting in glory atop Mount Zion. Observe the Jew on a donkey approaching the center of the Jewish universe and the abode of God. The holy city has become in his day a bastion of Roman power where Temple priests serve as pawns of Caesar.

As Jesus enters the city gate, see waving palm branches and hear crowds cry, "Hallelujah!" Through such gates as these, Roman generals enter defeated cities proclaiming the kingdom of Caesar, who as emperor is worshipped as a divine "Son of God" and "Savior" by order of the Roman Senate. On this day see, instead, a ragtag parade surrounding Jesus and announcing a kingdom of God. *Pax Dei* rather than *Pax Romana*. Yet rather than ascending a restored throne of the Jewish King David, Jesus will die the death of a political criminal.

Watch as Jesus goes first to the Temple. Inside see the tables of the money changers and of those who sell doves being tossed over. More than a "cleansing of the Temple," his symbolic move recalls the prophet Isaiah's judgment on those who turn a "house of prayer for all people" into what the prophet Jeremiah calls a "den of robbers." "Robber" priests in collusion with Rome are stealing hope from pilgrims held hostage to a priestly brokerage system at odds with the Torah's promise that sinners will be reconnected to God, the separation between them bridged, and what was torn asunder made one again.

It's a scene that calls to mind the moment of truth in *The Wizard of Oz*: Toto has grabbed the curtain and the horrible hoax is revealed for all to see. A price will be paid.

Reflect on religious and political places of power throughout history and in the world today as you imagine what Jerusalem and the Temple, the heart of political, military, and religious authority, represent for Jesus. Name thoughts, feelings, instincts, situations, and anything else that might draw Jesus there now. See him entering the city gates and imagine any hopes and fears, longings and apprehensions he may have in those moments.

- What does Jesus risk as he enters the city? What might finally going to Jerusalem promise him and his followers?

Look around to find and focus on the "Jerusalems" in your world.

- What is the heart of the matter in this country, or in your corporate world or neighborhood or community or congregation, that you circle around but are intent on avoiding or even denying for days, months, even years? What is your strategy for putting off and delaying ever going there?

Where between and among people like us is a Jerusalem that awaits our risking all by finally living and speaking out loud the truth? Ponder Jerusalems you have known in the past.

- When have you gone there? What had to happen finally to get you there?
- Over the years what strategies, tactics, detours, and diversions have you inherited, developed, depended on, and used to avoid going to Jerusalem?

Search your home, neighborhood, and country, and even your psyche and soul. Name a Jerusalem of yours that even now awaits your arrival. Consider the last place in the world you want to go, a place filled with both dread and promise, where although you will die there it is at the same time the only place you will ever come alive. Write something about your Jerusalem. Name your unfinished business. Identify the relationship with a person, a career, a persistent fear or ancient guilt, a shattered dream or broken promise, an addiction or obsession or a lie you are living—a bogus kind of security or comfort that keeps you captive to a charade. Going there to die is your only hope of living.

- How have you convinced yourself until now that there is no need to ever go there?
- Name the ways you continue to circle and avoid the Jerusalem that waits and will not go away.
- And as you circle and circle, what will it take for you to stop and then step through those gates?

Mirrors

There are some defeats more triumphant than victories.
    —Michel de Montaigne[94]

In my foolishness I did not know what I since have learnt: that the truth, even when it glorifies the human spirit, is hard to peddle if there is something terrible to tell as well. Dark nourishes light's triumphant blaze, but who should want to know? I accept, at last, that I am not to be allowed the mercy of telling what is mine to tell.
    —William Trevor, *A Bit on the Side: Stories*[95]

Listen to the different perceptions of September 11 around the world. Random, senseless violence, which can take loved ones at a moment's notice, is not a new experience for most of the world's people in places like Sarajevo, Johannesburg, or Jerusalem. Our illusions of invulnerability must be shattered—so we can join the rest of the world.
　　　　—Jim Wallis, *God's Politics: Why the Right Gets It Wrong and the Left Doesn't Get It*[96]

If suffering alone taught, all the world would be wise. . . . To suffering must be added mourning, understanding, patience, love, openness, and the willingness to remain vulnerable. All these and other factors combined, if the circumstances are right, can teach and can lead to rebirth.
　　　　—Anne Morrow Lindbergh, *Hours of Gold, Hours of Lead: Diaries and Lectures 1929–1973*[97]

The Well of Grief
by David Whyte[98]

> Those who will not slip beneath
> 　　the still surface of the well of grief
>
> turning downward through its black water
> 　　to the place we cannot breathe
>
> will never know the source from which we drink,
> 　　the secret water, cold and clear,
>
> nor find in the darkness glimmering
> 　　the small round coins
> 　　　　thrown by those who wished for something else.

Long Term
by Stephen Dunn[99]

> On this they were in agreement:
> everything that can happen between two people
> happens after a while
>
> or has been thought about so hard
> there's almost no difference
> between desire and deed.

Each day they stayed together, therefore,
was a day of forgiveness, tacit,
no reason to say the words.

It was easy to forgive, so much harder
to be forgiven. The forgiven had to agree
to eat dust in the house of the noble

and both knew this couldn't go on for long.
The forgiven would need to rise;
the forgiver need to remember the cruelty

in being correct.
Which is why, except in crises,
they spoke about the garden,
what happened at work,
the little ailments and aches
their familiar bodies separately felt.

FOURTEEN

BETRAYING TRUST

Then Judas Iscariot, who was one of the twelve, went to the chief priests in order to betray him to them. When they heard it, they were greatly pleased, and promised to give him money. So he began to look for an opportunity to betray him.

Immediately, while he was still speaking, Judas, one of the twelve, arrived; and with him there was a crowd with swords and clubs, from the chief priests, the scribes, and the elders. Now the betrayer had given them a sign, saying, "The one I will kiss is the man; arrest him and lead him away under guard." So when he came, he went up to him at once and said, "Rabbi!" and kissed him. Then they laid hands on him and arrested him. (Mark 14:10–11, 43–46)

Reflections
BY CAREN

Shortly after moving to Northampton, Massachusetts, in 2004, I discovered that folk in this lively New England city tend to wear their hearts on their sleeves when they protest humanity's inhumanity to humanity. Sometimes such passionate protests take the form of peaceful pickets. Other times silent vigils. Occasionally a parade. Today it is a long string of "dirty" laundry that encircles a spacious verdant quad on the site of the city's most famous institution: Smith College.

As the largest liberal arts college for women in the country, as well as an academic powerhouse, Smith attracts twenty-five hundred of the most intellectual, creative, and promising students from around the world to its campus. Besides being highly invested in their education, many of the women are also dedicated to making a difference in others' lives. They volunteer their services to nonprofits serving the community and stand up publicly to speak truth to the abuses of local, national, and international powers.

Today, the Clothesline Project that uses T-shirts to bear witness to violence against women and sexually abused children expresses one of the students' many collective concerns. It encircles a campus quad where seemingly hundreds of the T-shirts created by these women and their friends and relatives flutter in a breeze like colorful Tibetan peace flags. T-shirts with designer labels and no labels, saying "Never forget" and "We shall overcome" to the physical, psychological, emotional, and spiritual costs of betrayals named rape, incest, domestic violence, boundary violations, and child sexual abuse.

> "You beat mom and me for years, but you can't hurt us anymore, Daddy, you can't hurt us anymore."
> "Rape took away more than my virginity."
> "You're in jail for raping me, but I'm serving a life sentence."
> "Grandpa, every night you came into that bedroom, you became my worst nightmare. @#%$•\^#@^&^%#!!!"
> "Mom, why didn't you protect me? Why didn't you stop it?"
> "You were supposed to be my therapist—not my lover."
> "I'm sorry I didn't protect you, sis. He was doing me, too."
> "Never again will you have that power over me!"
> "You stole more than my heart."

Fifty-eight thousand men died in the Vietnam War. During that same period, the Clothesline Project reports, fifty-one thousand women were killed—mostly by men who had offered them their undying love. Like most people drawn to this temporary testament to that truth, I walk slowly and silently while reading each T-shirt. Three women—a mother and two daughters—pass by. They look anxious, pained, and puzzled as they scan the laundry instead of reading it. Their faces say what their voices don't: "It has to be here somewhere." At last one of them points. Together they walk toward that which has awaited them. Six eyes begin moving as one to read and read again their personal patch of red cotton. Finished, they silently stand stunned. As their searching eyes slowly connect and mirror each other's feelings, the mother folds to the ground. Her daughters kneel down to embrace her. And together they sob and they sob and they wail.

The tears that fall from our eyes and fill our souls after a betrayal by a loved and trusted one can be among the heaviest of all. When they come, they pop out rhythmically to nonstop pounding in our heads and hearts. They swell and stream in response to every acknowledgment of how much we've been stung, taken for granted, violated, trespassed upon, and knocked out by a magnum force blow we couldn't or just didn't see coming. The forcefulness of such tears reddens our eyes with a flood of the emotional debris that can accompany intractable pain, confusion, loss, and a desire for revenge. They bathe our cheeks, lips, jawlines, necks, and laps in primeval salt water that reawakens our reptilian instinct to fight or flee. And from a well that feels bottomless, they flow and they flow, unpredictably and on their own schedule, to douse us with surprise, embarrassment, and a ceaseless desire to make sense out of nonsense. Such tears remind us that once we witness something, it cannot be unwitnessed—that when a part of our life dies, it really is dead.

"How could this have happened," a dear friend asked after discovering her husband's affair with a close friend.

"Why didn't I see this coming?" my uncle wondered after his business partner swindled him out of his life savings.

"Where did I first screw up?" a father demanded to know during a fruitless search for his runaway daughter.

At some time—because there's always a first time—all of us learn that betrayal wears many guises and usually shows up dressed as those closest to us—those whom we love and trust, those whom we were convinced we might even die for. It also shows up as our most trusted and beloved leaders, and sometimes it even shows up as ourselves. No surprise, then, that betrayal always has the power to strip us of our beliefs, dignity, and self-worth and make us feel vulnerable, culpable, guilty, shameful, out of control, and lifeless.

Walking the quad for the second time, I feel exhausted from reading T-shirts, from looking at the pain on the faces of those around and beside me, and from my psyche and soul hurting. Many of the stories told by this stream of "dirty" laundry are my story, too.

I walk away feeling grief and remorse that will endure. Grief and remorse as one who has been betrayed. Grief and remorse for all those whom I have consciously and unconsciously betrayed along the way. Yet I also feel that something within has been empowered to say "Yes" to healing by being more—much more—than betrayals past that still have an unpredictable power to sting, overwhelm, wound, depress, cause nightmares and post-traumatic stress, and push buttons that release heavy tears.

Before turning a corner, I look back at the Clothesline Project to see spaces where I could hang my dirty laundry. Moving on I know that betrayal will remain a dense, dark cloud hanging over the project and parts of my life. It doesn't have a sunny side. But in its disturbing and disruptive wake, it does illuminate: it does illuminate a side of my shadow that I could never see otherwise.

Wanderings and Wonderings

Whether you are reading these Scripture passages for the first time or for the hundredth, read them again with a director's, novelist's, or detective's eye. Assume that your task is to bring Judas to life in a movie, story, or play. Begin by writing down your description of Jesus' betrayer, whose name literally means "Jewish man."

According to the gospel stories, Judas is a disciple of Jesus but also a man the chief priests and elders can buy for a price. In Matthew's story that bounty equals thirty pieces of silver. What facial characteristics or expressions help make your interpretation of one named Judas come alive? What about his build, his stance, his clothes, his movements, his mannerisms, or the tone of his voice? If you have a copy of the New Testament, compare the stories in Mark, Matthew, Luke, and John, and wonder what you would want your audience to know, experience, and feel about Judas's incentive to hand Jesus over to the authorities.

Without going to a dictionary, write down your definition of the word *betray*. Now add words and phrases to your attempt as a director, novelist, or detective to bring Judas to life. You might also draw pictures or cut them out of a newspaper or magazine to create a montage that expands your view of Judas. Now sit quietly with your characterization of this one who betrays in front of you. Continue to add anything else that makes your "picture" of Judas complete.

Although there are no recorded accounts of Judas's ancestral lineage, for over two thousand years his role in the gospel stories has been defined by one word: *betrayer*. Once again look at your picture of Judas and your definition of *betray*. Judas's betrayal is sealed by a kiss. Indeed, some translate the original Greek not as "and he kissed him," but as "he kissed him much."

- What more might Judas's kiss tell you about the thoughts, feelings, and concerns of one who betrays Jesus?
- And what does that kiss say to you about other betrayals sealed with such intimacy?

From the first time Judas appears in the gospel narratives, he is labeled a betrayer. However, Judas is not the only one whose actions may have betrayed Jesus. For example, some would say the disciples betray Jesus by falling asleep in Gethsemane instead of honoring his request to "watch and pray that you may not enter temptation." Others point out that Peter, in particular, betrays Jesus when he denies him three times. Could the fact that the disciples flee when Jesus is arrested also be considered a betrayal? And what about their choice not to show up at Jesus' crucifixion? And finally, is it possible that even God may betray Jesus by not showing up at Jesus' arrest, trial, and crucifixion?

While considering whether Judas is the only one to betray Jesus, use your historical imagination. Be Judas and stand before Jesus. Look at him curiously as one who is stirring many feelings inside. Acknowledge what you see and feel. Then ask yourself, is it possible that Judas acts as he does because he feels as though Jesus has betrayed *him*?

Shift gears and look far beyond wherever you may be sitting or standing. Name those leaders of our political, financial, educational, and religious institutions who you feel betray our country, communities, families, and you.

- What form do such betrayals by those in power take?
- Have you ever intuited such a betrayal before it happened?
- If so, what kept you from believing it, acting on it, or preventing it?
- And what do you still want to say or do in the moments, hours, and days after you knew beyond a doubt that those leaders had betrayed you?

Recall a time of feeling betrayed by a family member, lover, partner, mentor, or close friend.

- Did you see it coming?
- How did you feel, react, or respond?
- What was the outcome?

Recall a time when another said or implied that you betrayed him or her. If you agree that a betrayal took place, consider the following:

- What did you hope—consciously or unconsciously—to change, transform, or revenge when the betrayal occurred?
- Was your betrayal the result of an impulsive action or a calculated one?

Whether you were driven or compelled to betray another, once your actions were labeled, they introduced you to someone in your psyche, and perhaps your soul, named "Judas."

- How did you "kiss" the other?
- How would you describe the havoc your Judas wrought?
- What subsequent violence, passion, and "death" did your betrayal precipitate?
- How might your life be different today if you had resisted "thirty pieces of silver" or some other temptation that your Judas accepted?
- What did you want or need or expect from the one whom you betrayed that you could not give to yourself?

In a later chapter, Matthew follows up on Judas's story and tells us that in his grief and under the burden of his guilt, Judas returns to the Temple and throws the silver down before the chief priests and elders. He then departs and hangs himself.

As you look back on a personal act of betrayal, ask yourself:

- What have I killed, punished, or even sacrificed as Judas did in hopes of atoning, making it right, and easing the burden of my guilt?
- When, where, and how did this event reveal that I might also have betrayed myself?
- What did betrayal of another and possibly myself invite into my life that could not have entered any other way?
- And what remains enlightened by this betrayal that would otherwise remain in the dark?

Mirrors

Every person needs to sense the evil in them not as literal destructiveness but as a necessary and ultimately beneficial capacity for the dark. Actual evil deeds are merely a sign that this evil hasn't been taken to heart in a refined way, and therefore has to be acted out.
    —Thomas Moore[100]

We are led to an essential truth about both trust and betrayal: they contain each other. You cannot have trust without the possibility of betrayal. . . . We are betrayed in the very same close relationships where primal trust is possible. We can be truly betrayed only where we truly trust—by brothers,

lovers, wives, husbands, not by enemies, not by strangers. The greater the love and loyalty, the involvement and commitment, the greater the betrayal.
    —James Hillman, *Loose Ends*[101]

No man consciously chooses evil because it is evil; he only mistakes it for the happiness that he seeks.
    —Mary Wollstonecraft Shelley[102]

> Ring the bells that still can ring,
> Forget your perfect offering.
> There is a crack in everything.
> That's how the light gets in.
>   —Leonard Cohen, "Anthem"[103]

From *The Gulag Archipelago 1918–1956*
by Aleksandr Isaevich Solzhenitsyn[104]

If it were all so simple! If only there were evil people somewhere insidiously committing evil deeds, and it were necessary only to separate them from the rest of us and destroy them. But the line dividing good and evil cuts through the heart of every human being. And who is willing to destroy a piece of his own heart?

During the life of any heart this line keeps changing place; sometimes it is squeezed one way by exuberant evil and sometimes it shifts to allow enough space for good to flourish. One and the same human being is, at various ages, under various circumstances, a totally different human being. At times he is close to being a devil, at times to sainthood. But his name doesn't change, and to that name we ascribe the whole lot, good and evil. Socrates taught us: Know thyself!

Confronted by the pit into which we are about to toss those who have done us harm, we halt, stricken dumb: it is after all only because of the way things worked out that they were the executioners and we weren't.

The Book
by Linda Pastan[105]

> In the book of shadows
> the first page is dark
> and the second darker still,
> but on the next page,
> and the next, there is a flickering

as if the shadows are dancing
with themselves, as if they are dancing
with the leaves they mimic.
Before Narcissus found the pool
it was his shadow he loved,

the way we grow to love our deaths
when we meet them
in dreams. For as we turn
the pages of the book
each page grows heavier
under our numbed fingers, and only
the shadows themselves
are weightless,
only the shadows welcome us
beneath their cool canopy.

ONE: The Portrait
by Stanley Kunitz[106]

My mother never forgave my father
for killing himself,
especially at such an awkward time
and in a public park,
that spring
when I was waiting to be born.
She locked his name
in her deepest cabinet
and would not let him out,
though I could hear him thumping.
When I came down from the attic
with the pastel portrait in my hand
of a long-lipped stranger
with a brave moustache
and deep brown level eyes,
she ripped it into shreds
without a single word
and slapped me hard.
In my sixty-fourth year
I can feel my cheek
still burning.

In a Dark Time
by Theodore Roethke[107]

> In a dark time, the eye begins to see,
> I meet my shadow in the deepening shade;
> I hear my echo in the echoing wood—
> A lord of nature weeping to a tree.
> I live between the heron and the wren,
> Beasts of the hill and serpents of the den.
>
> What's madness but nobility of soul
> At odds with circumstance? The day's on fire!
> I know the purity of pure despair,
> My shadow pinned against a sweating wall.
> That place among the rocks—is it a cave,
> Or winding path? The edge is what I have.
>
> A steady storm of correspondences!
> A night flowing with birds, a ragged moon,
> And in broad day the midnight come again!
> A man goes far to find out what he is—
> Death of the self in a long, tearless night,
> All natural shapes blazing unnatural light.
>
> Dark, dark my light, and darker my desire.
> My soul, like some heat-maddened summer fly,
> Keeps buzzing at the sill. Which I is I?
> A fallen man, I climb out of my fear.
> The mind enters itself, and God the mind,
> And one is One, free in the tearing wind.

FIFTEEN

EPILOGUE: BREEDING NEW ALGEBRAS

"Good Teacher, what must I do to inherit eternal life?" Jesus said to him, "Why do you call me good? No one is good but God alone. You know the commandments: 'You shall not murder; You shall not commit adultery; You shall not steal; You shall not bear false witness; You shall not defraud; Honor your father and mother.'" He said to him, "Teacher, I have kept all these since my youth." Jesus, looking at him, loved him and said, "You lack one thing; go, sell what you own, and give the money to the poor, and you will have treasure in heaven; then come, follow me." When he heard this, he was shocked and went away grieving, for he had many possessions. (Mark 10:17–22)

The kingdom of God is like a woman who was carrying a jar full of meal. While she was walking along a distant road, the handle of the jar broke and the meal spilled behind her along the road. She didn't know it; she hadn't noticed the problem. When she reached her house, she put the jar down and discovered that it was empty. (*Gospel of Thomas* 97)

Reflections
BY BILL

Early one morning, one year to the day, I turn on the television to discover the footprint of the twin towers occupied by only a large circle. In the hours to follow, the space fills with the grieving families of those who died and with them the president of the United States. The circle becomes carpeted with flowers brought as symbols of hope. But for the moment, there is no one. Nothing. Only a large empty circle. A giant silent zero.

In his poem "A Hard Death," Amos Wilder writes:

> Accept no mitigation,
> But be instructed at the null point.
> The zero breeds new algebras.[108]

Null points are where hope ends and dreams die in a marriage or career or simply in a broken heart longing for meaning, purpose, security, peace, or even love. And now, in the wake of the null point that will always be referred to as 9/11, we know as a nation what each of us has experienced in the darkest shadows of our lives. It is there, Wilder tells us, at the zero places of null and nothing that new algebras are discovered. And once there, he advises, "accept no mitigation"—those strategies we devise to avoid, diminish, or deny the null points in our lives. Yet despite the emptiness, disorientation, and feeling of existential death we experience at our personal ground zeroes, the truth is that those particular null points become *the* places where new ways of counting and computing, reading our lives, and making sense of the world happen.

As the story goes in the gospel of Mark, a man who may be at such a null point runs up to and kneels before Jesus. In search of a life that is eternal, enduring, and lasting—not ephemeral or fleeting—he hopes for a new algebra.

Initially, the story focuses on the commandments and the man's claim that he has kept them since childhood. Jesus then tells him that he therefore lacks but one thing. He must go, sell all, and give the money to the poor. However, upon hearing that shocking injunction, the man goes away sorrowful—"grieving, for he had many possessions."

One possible end to the story is that emptying his treasury was too much for the man to even consider. On the other hand, nothing is said about him *not* embracing the one thing he lacks, which, ironically, may be to have nothing. The young man may simply begin his new algebra by grieving. For him, riches equate with money. Our coffers, however, may be filled with different treasures that take the form of success, ego, control, fears, fantasies, pride, talent, status, purity, or even badges of abuse. We are rich with whatever we hold on to as if our life depends on it. Even when it is killing us.

The *Gospel of Thomas* is a collection of 114 sayings of Jesus discovered in 1945 at Nag Hammadi in Egypt. Scholars debate the source and date of the writings, but none deny that eleven of the fourteen parables in the ancient text parallel those found in Matthew, Mark, and Luke. One that is not parallel tells of a woman with a jar. While walking a distant road, all her meal leaks out. Since not enough time has passed for theologians and preachers to analyze, interpret, and then teach us what Jesus really meant, we can encounter the bewilderment and mystery first-century Jews may have experienced on hearing the parable for the first time.

For some, the kingdom of God referred to in *Thomas* is what spills out along the road from the broken jar, the moral is to be conscious and stay alert or we, too, will lose it. For others this is a story about how the kingdom of God is spread about the world without our even knowing it. Another possibility: the kingdom of God is about something else. The kingdom of God is, perhaps, precisely what the text says: a woman arrives home to find the jar empty. Intuitively, we sense that had the woman known what was happening, noticed the problem, she most likely would have scrambled to repair the jar, recover the meal, avoid the emptiness, and then feel relieved to carry on with business as usual. Instead, as if things were normal, she journeys home unaware, until she discovers that her plenty, her more than enough, is suddenly and unexpectedly null and void.

An empty jar is what the moment feels like when each of us suddenly becomes aware that that which matters most—and on which we have gambled all—has spilled, leaked out, washed away, and been forever lost from our marriages or life work or fondest hopes and bravest dreams.

Jesus is not talking to the rich young man about regrets. He is telling the one who yearns for life, as we do, that it is a gift for the taking that costs not less than everything. Embracing the gift begins by coming home to self from our journey on distant roads to discover the sadness and wonder of an empty jar. Tears of grief over broken nations and ended relationships, wrecked hopes and shattered dreams, prepare us for new possibilities that can happen in no other way. It is a life, perhaps for the first time, open to more. Essayist and poet Barbara Hurd writes:

> In Tibetan Buddhism, the word "shul" means the impression left when something has passed through. A cave carved out by water. A footprint in the mud. The enormous white space that opens when you stop clinging to what you think will protect you, whether it's love or success. The unguarded void that remains when you realize you're mortal, the clearing into which insight can move and some other voice can be heard. We need, it seems, some absence in order to feel the presence of something larger. Monks use the word "shul" to mean the holy path of emptiness they travel. And in Yiddish, the word means temple.[109]

In Mark 16:1–8, the following story is told:

When the sabbath was over, Mary Magdalene, and Mary the mother of James, and Salome bought spices, so that they might go and anoint him. And very early on the first day of the week, when the sun had risen, they went to the tomb. They had been saying to one another, "Who will roll away the stone for us from the entrance to the tomb?" When they looked up, they saw that the stone, which was very large, had already been rolled back. As they entered the tomb, they saw a young man, dressed in a white robe, sitting on the right side; and they were alarmed. But he said to them, "Do not be alarmed; you are looking for Jesus of Nazareth, who was crucified. He has been raised; he is not here. Look, there is the place they laid him. But go, tell his disciples and Peter that he is going ahead of you to Galilee; there you will see him, just as he told you." So they went out and fled from the tomb, for terror and amazement had seized them; and they said nothing to anyone, for they were afraid.

Jesus' dying on a cross is a grim reminder that when one chooses to live life with authenticity, as Jesus chose to live his, a price will be paid. Both in society and in psyche—privately and publicly—there is a high cost to speaking truth in the face of life-threatening oppression. Saying yes to the kind of life described in the Jesus stories in this book means dying to much of what we have been taught to value and believe, as well as to much of our natural instinct for self-preservation, comfort, and survival.

The epilogue to the life of the man named Jesus is a story of an empty tomb. No matter what you call it—Easter or Resurrection or something similar in other religious traditions—it is an expression of an archetypal and universal experience rather than a belief or creedal assent. When we are graced with what Jesus calls "faith" in these stories, new life rises out of death again and again as we weather our storms, stand up straight after years of looking at the ground, and discover the mysterious and amazing possibility of experiencing rebirth in those empty, null, zero places of our days. It is a life promise made to us no matter what tomb we haunt and inhabit. Like the women, we say little because it is fearful to find in Jesus' life the bold assertion that it is in dying that we finally discover the healing and eternal life that hovers and waits for us here and now.

Wanderings and Wonderings

Yearning, loss, emptiness, and death—unplanned feelings and uncomfortable occasions that invite us to step outside the box and beyond our horizon in hopes of discovering our paths to healing and wholeness. Along the way, we may find many who help point us in those directions. For some it is Abraham, Moses, Buddha, Muhammad, or others. On this particular journey, the person pointing a way to an authentic life has been a Jewish man named Jesus.

As you read and re-read the chapters containing the stories of your life, continue to let questions about your truth guide you. Wonder about the time you ran after and knelt before someone you hoped might tell you where to find a life that is deep and enduring.

Look out your window and see a woman on a distant road far from home carrying a broken jar from which meal spills along the road:

- Where is she and what is happening to her?
- How can this loss occur without her noticing it?
- If she were aware of what is happening, what might she do?
- And how might this change the end of the story?

See yourself walking along a distant road far from home, carrying whatever you have that is most valuable to you. As you head home, the jar holding this treasure breaks, but you're oblivious to it. You keep walking as the contents you depend on steadily leak out. Finally, you reach home, put the jar down, and discover that your container is empty.

- How does your container get broken?
- Moreover, how does that which you have made to matter the most leak out without your knowing it?
- In what way might the surprise of discovering your jar is empty be an essential part of arriving home?

Recall Barbara Hurd's description of a holy path of emptiness (see p. 114) and see if you can locate the *shul* or temple in your life. Scan your inner and outer worlds to determine what cave carved out of water has imprisoned you and held you hostage for three days or longer.

- Where is your "enormous white space, the unguarded void, the clearing"?
- Where around and deep within you might a different kind of *temple* be waiting?

Each of the stories about Jesus and the people and situations he encountered from day one mirrors our life stories, too. The characters are but reflections of the dramas we live between and deep within each of us. Consequently, at different times and in different places, they get tightly woven into the tapestry of committed relationships and family, days on the job or in the office. They become the warp and woof, the threads of our beliefs and certainties, faiths and convictions, worries and fears. These stories even get woven into our anticipation of our unavoidable death.

- What is the tomb that holds you prisoner?
- How are you walking around lifeless in the dark in search of life?
- What is the fear that seals the bargain you make between being safe and staying dead?

Looking back on the stories about Jesus of Nazareth whom you have found in the pages of this book, contemplate new possibilities for discovering more of your whole self that have become apparent. Theologian and author Harvey Cox writes:

> The philosopher Alasdair MacIntyre has suggested that the only way to answer the question, "What am I to do?" is to ask, "Of what story or stories do I find myself a part?" Stories do that. They start the mind and memory racing. They spark connections and associations. They recall similar experiences in the life of the hearer.[110]

Like all of our lives, your life is an unfinished book containing chapters filled with stories, and you, too, have an epilogue that waits to be written.

- What is the null point in your life today? Where is the zero waiting to teach you new algebras? What must be sold, lost, or die on your way to learning a different way to compute your life and to discover a new way to live your days?

What is the first sentence in the story of the rest of your life?

The kindest thing anyone could have done for me, once I'd finished five weeks' radiation, would have been to look me square in the eye and say this clearly, "Reynolds Price is dead. Who will you be now? Who can you be and how can you get there, double time? . . . Come back to life, whoever you'll be."
>   —Reynolds Price, *A Whole New Life: An Illness and
>   a Healing*[111]

The most difficult of the dinner parties I ruin are usually around Christmas, and always those of the younger members of the firm, who, no matter how well they have done, have yet to find their place because they have yet to fall from grace and restore themselves. They know I have built and rebuilt, that, quite apart from my military history, I have, in corporate terms, come back from the dead. That very thing, though I did not ask for it, is what they fear the most to get and fear the most in me.

    —Mark Helprin, *The Pacific and Other Stories*[112]

True myths may serve for thousands of years as an inexhaustible source of intellectual speculation, religious joy, ethical inquiry, and artistic renewal. The real mystery is not destroyed by reason. The fake one is. You look at it and it vanishes. You look at the Blond Hero—really look—and he turns into a gerbil. But you look at Apollo and he looks back at you. The poet Rilke looked at a statue of Apollo about fifty years ago, and Apollo spoke to him. "You must change your life," he said. When the true myth rises into consciousness, that is always its message: "You must change your life."

    —Ursula K. LeGuin, from *Sunbeams: A Book of Quotations*
    by Sy Syfransky[113]

To lose. To have lost. I believed these visitations of darkness lasted only a few minutes or hours and that these saddened people, in between bouts, were occupied, as we all were, with the useful monotony of happiness. But happiness is not what I thought. Happiness is the lucky pane of glass you carry in your head. It takes all your cunning just to hang on to it, and once it's smashed you have to move into a different sort of life.

    —Carol Shields, *Unless*[114]

From *Age of Iron*
by J. M. Coetzee[115]

"It is a confession I am making here, this morning," I said, "as full a confession as I know how. I withhold no secrets. I have been a good person, I freely confess to it. I am a good person still. What times these are when to be a good person is not enough!

    "What I had not calculated on was that more might be called for than to be good. For there are plenty of good people in this country. We are two a penny, we good and nearly good. What the times call for is quite different than goodness. The times call for heroism. A word that, as I speak it, sounds foreign to my lips. I doubt that I have ever used it before, even in a lecture. Why not? Perhaps out of respect. Perhaps out of shame. As one drops one's gaze before one standing naked."

A Man Lost by a River
by Michael Blumenthal[116]

There is a voice inside the body.

There is a voice and a music,
a throbbing, four-chambered pear
that wants to be heard, that sits
alone by the river with its mandolin
and its torn coat, and sings
to whomever will listen
a song that no one wants to hear.

But sometimes, lost,
on his way to somewhere significant,
a man in a long coat, carrying
a briefcase, wanders into the forest.

He hears the voice and the mandolin,
he sees the thrush and the dandelion,
and he feels the mist rise over the river.

And his life is never the same,
for this having been lost—
for having strayed from the path of his routine,
for no good reason.

From *The Velveteen Rabbit*
by Margery Williams[117]

"What is REAL?" asked the Rabbit one day. . . . "Does it happen all at once like being wound up, or bit by bit?"

"It doesn't happen all at once," said the Skin Horse. "You become. It takes a long time. That's why it doesn't often happen to people who break easily, or have sharp edges, or have to be carefully kept. Generally, by the time you are Real, most of your hair has been loved off, and your eyes drop out and you get loose in the joints and very shabby. But these things don't matter at all, because once you are Real you can't be ugly, except to people who don't understand."

ENDPAPERS

It is I who must begin. Once I begin, once I try—here and now, right where I am, not excusing myself by saying that things would be easier elsewhere, without grand speeches and ostentatious gestures, but all the more persistently—to live in harmony with the "voice of Being," as I understand it within myself—as soon as I begin that, I suddenly discover, to my surprise, that I am neither the only one, nor the first, nor the most important one to have set out upon that road. For the hope opened in my heart by this turning toward Being has opened my eyes as well to all the hopeful things my vision, blinded by the brilliance of "worldly" temptations, could not or did not wish to see, because it would have undermined the traditional argument of all those who have given up already: that all is lost anyway. Whether all is really lost or not depends entirely on whether or not I am lost.

—Vaclav Havel, *Letters to Olga*[118]

Caren

I am Jewish, and like many children of the Diaspora who were raised in the shadow of the Holocaust, my parents told me that Hitler and Jesus were personally responsible for the deaths of millions of innocent Jews. Therefore neither name should ever—never ever—be spoken inside our house. They really meant it. Merely muttering "Jeez-sus" or thoughtlessly exclaiming "For Christ's sake!" resulted in my mouth getting washed with soap. As a result, I never risked asking questions about Jesus, which is just as well. No one in my house or neighborhood would have known the answers.

I spent most of my childhood in Brooklyn, New York, believing that the borderline religious education I received was a norm for Jews everywhere. Like many secular Jews, we always attended Rosh Hashonah and Yom Kippur services at nearby synagogues. None ever really served as a home base. We also lit Chanukah candles and drove over to Grandma and Grandpa Goldman's for the first night of Passover. On the second night we strolled over to Nana and Grandpa Rosenstock's. And there you have it. That was the extent of my family's connection to our religious past with one exception—our semi-strict observance of Judaism's dietary laws. Upstairs in our house, the kitchen was kosher—just like the kitchens of every generation of Goldmans and Rosenstocks. That meant that we could not mix dishes, pots, pans, and fine silverware for meat and for dairy products. They never found their way to the same table and were stored in separate cabinets and drawers. The same was true for extra sets of plates, pots, utensils, and miscellany for the eight days of Passover.

However, in the basement, it was another story. There, hidden in red leather padded benches that lined pine-paneled walls, was yet one more set of dishes and cheap stainless steel for the Chinese takeout that became a Sunday dinner ritual. On that night, which was very different from all others, my mother would bring out a card table, cover it with a red and white checkered cloth, and set it with plates, spoons, forks, knives, and chopsticks while my father went to pick up his standing order. Back home, Dad would reenter the house through the cellar door followed by the familiar scent of a forbidden feast wafting after him. Watching him unpack brown paper bags filled with white boxes decorated with intriguing red pictograms down the side was almost as exciting as the contents they contained. Finally, the moment would arrive when we could begin slurping egg drop soup, chomping on chow mein, and savoring shrimpless fried rice. Never, in my memory, had even one matzo ball been held in such high esteem. Not until years later, in the midst of leading a "Finding Jesus" seminar, did I realize that whenever we dined out inside our small home in Brooklyn, I was being fed my first lessons in the ways those closest to me made choices about the letter of the law.

Ultimately, my parents' highest priority as first-generation American Jews was to assimilate in the post–World War II and Holocaust era. My task was to follow in their footsteps and absorb my religious heritage by osmosis. Years later when people would ask me, "What religion are you?" I'd sometimes answer, "Skewish."

Not until my parents agreed, fearfully, to allow me to get my journalism degree from a renowned department in a Methodist university in the Midwest did I begin to risk asking myself questions about this mysterious person named Jesus. "Might he be someone other than the stereotypical portrait that Christianity has painted on one canvas and Judaism on another?" I wondered. However, old gag orders die hard.

Despite being five hundred miles from home, I could still taste soap whenever the "J" word slipped past my lips. So instead of seeking answers from the noted biblical scholars on campus, I cached my list of questions about Jesus in a hidden vault in my mind. And that's where they remained for almost two decades.

An urge to know more about Jesus came during an early midlife crisis. At the time, I was a divorced parent who had decided to leave a long-term relationship. As though that choice wasn't stressful enough, I also exited my nine-to-five job as the assistant editor at a weekly Jewish newspaper and returned to freelancing full-time—a risky venture at best. To help bridge the gap between the secure world I was choosing to leave and the wilderness that seemed to be calling me, I signed up for the rugged eleven-day Outward Bound sailing expedition off the coast of Maine described in chapter 3. Outward Bound challenges participants to acknowledge and overcome self-imposed limitations by meeting them head-on in the outdoors. Exercises that are physically and emotionally demanding become literal and metaphorical vehicles that drive participants to explore new paradigms for their lives and their relationships. "You're nuts," a friend proclaimed when I told her. "It's something twenty-year-olds do, not forty-year-olds." I agreed with her and went anyway.

Sitting on the lawn during OB orientation, I introduced myself to the "Bounder" next to me. "What do you do?" I asked.

"I'm an Episcopal priest," Ted Voorhees answered.

"An Episcopal *priest*? What's that?" I asked.

In the days that followed, Ted gave me a short course in Episcopal Church life. He also explained that he was on sabbatical and had just returned from attending a seventeen-day seminar called "The Records of the Life of Jesus" in Northern California. It was offered by the Guild for Psychological Studies, a group dedicated to enabling participants to discover their own unique value system and inner authority and to enhance their ability to make mature choices. The experiential event at an isolated three-hundred-acre mountainside retreat center focused on a comparative study of passages in the New Testament gospels of Mark, Matthew, and Luke. The seminar also drew from mythology, depth psychology, and the expressive arts, and the leaders made it clear there was no need or obligation to come to a consensus about what those first-century writings meant.

Thus, as I began to view Jesus through the wide lens Ted offered me, I began to see the forbidden one differently and broaden my assumptions. Not only was Jesus a Jewish wisdom keeper, a choice maker, and a risk taker who had an extraordinary sense of self; he was also someone who had possibly been surrounded, hidden, and perhaps smothered by thick layers of theology and dogma for generations.

Slowly, my interest escalated in the first-century Jewish man whom Ted described, especially when he admitted, "For the first time I'm really beginning to live the unconventional questions that I had about Jesus long before I went to seminary."

"Live questions?" I said to myself. "He says he's a priest. If he doesn't have an array of answers, who does?"

Ted continued, "While looking at these texts to discover what Jesus might have really said instead of what others say about him, I began to live questions that clergy, seminary professors, and others told me not to ask and refused to answer. Questions that made them feel uncomfortable. Questions that made them question my faith and my integrity. The whole time the leaders of this seminar affirmed the fact that it was okay *not* to have answers and that I could live as long as I wanted—even a lifetime—pondering questions and feeling ambiguous about who Jesus, a first-century Jew, might have been. It also reinforced my belief that it's possible that many of the events of Jesus' life might never have happened."

"What if they didn't happen?" I asked.

Rather than offer an answer, Ted just asked another question. "What do you believe? Are the stories in the Torah literal and historical, or are they just stories that contain timeless truths?"

Immediately, I opened my mouth to reply. But then thought otherwise. "I need to ponder *my* answer," I said hesitantly. "I don't believe it's a case of either/or. As a matter of fact, I think I'm beginning to understand what you mean by 'live the questions.'"

And pondering is just what I've been doing for the last eighteen years—first as a Jew and a Jewish journalist. Later as a seeker, who went to California to take "The Records" and then went on to become both a facilitator of that process and the Jewish wife of an Episcopal priest named Ted. And finally, as someone who discovered along the way that by learning to live questions and love doing so, my spiritual journey has become a healing one. Now those separate paintings of Judaism and Christianity I mentioned earlier look different to me—radically different. Now questions about what Jesus' spiritual journey tells me, a practicing Jew, about being a mature and healthy choice maker both enlighten and strengthen me in my quest to become an authentic self with an ever-deepening relationship to Judaism and the Divine. Now I can feel safe asking myself the question, what might it mean to take seriously what Jesus, the Jew, took seriously, and not have it become confused with a different question that asks, what might it mean to take seriously what Christianity has taken seriously for almost two thousand years?

In *Finding Jesus, Discovering Self*, Bill Dols and I have invited you to engage in a unique process that explores the Gospels—a process we hope doesn't end here but will always be available. First to help you learn to "live the questions." And then to help you begin to choose to take steps outside your "box," no matter what your religious background or spiritual beliefs may be—or not be.

Throughout these pages, it was our intention to give you tools and resources that can serve as a multifaceted lens to help you explore two-thousand-year-old stories with new eyes. My hope is that in the process, you not only saw new questions raised by the timeless stories about Jesus, but perhaps learned to love living those questions, too. And finally, it is my hope that the questions you pondered and continue to live will not only lead you to new discoveries and universal truths about your life and the world around you, but remain a welcome signpost on your journey to healing and wholeness.

Bill

In this climate-controlled, air-conditioned world, I forget how hot and humid it could get in August in Baltimore in the 1930s. Deep into the nights of those dog days of summer, the city would become a mosaic of front stoop and porch sitters longing for just a wisp of a breeze. Radnor Avenue glowed with the glisten of cigarettes burning everywhere. Sounds drifted in the dark, carrying soft talk, gentle laughter, and now and then, distant radio music. And on one such night, for a small child up way past bedtime and nestled between Mom and Dad on a creaking porch swing, it was more magic than hot. When I finally wearied, my father gently picked me up, cradled me in his arms, and carried me into the house and up the stairs to my bed. Today, that moment lingers as my earliest childhood memory.

The rest of the story is about seventy years of longing to be embraced by those secure, loving arms during the darkness that comes with long, stifling nights of the soul. From my earliest years I sought those strong arms by achieving and pleasing, being a good boy who worked hard and kept the rules, while keeping most feelings and thoughts to myself. I learned to do things rather well, which led pleased adults to speak graciously about me and reward me with their esteem. Even when I was young, the abiding issue in my story was the tension between pretense and performance as opposed to presence and truth. Early on I found that the world values performing and pretending more highly than expressions of yearnings and fears. When my mother was very angry with me, she would say in a huff, "If they could only see you at home!" Early on I learned that knowing how to dissemble and disguise was the secret.

From the start, I believe, my longing for embracing arms had everything to do with God. Mention of God in our house was limited largely to my father's mumbled words "in Christ's name" before dinner. And the times when my grandmother closed her bedroom door, showed me her rosary, and talked of her daily visit to a Roman Catholic church on the way to work at Lane Bryant's. My mother said bedtime prayers with me. I remember best the part about "if I should die before I wake."

The church's promise of welcoming arms began at the Episcopal cathedral in a children's chapel with undersized furniture painted green. Jesus, portrayed as a serene and happy little boy surrounded by deer and birds, looked down at me from above the altar. Years later when asked why I devoted so much energy to the efforts to ordain women priests, I immediately recalled Louise Jose, the tall and stately white-haired Sunday school teacher who was also my priest and bishop at five years old. Miss Jose selected who would collect the offering in the gold-painted wooden box with seraphim on the top and who would light and extinguish candles. To get chosen took no little pretending and performing.

After Sunday school kindergarten, I joined the men and boys' choir, vested every Sunday morning in a black robe, white cotta, and huge black bow tied by the choir mother. A move to the choir of Old St. Paul's Church downtown in the seventh grade qualified me to attend a private church school more famous for lacrosse than academics. It seemed like the obvious thing not long thereafter to go to Washington and Lee University, when offered a scholarship, and then on to the Virginia Theological Seminary in Alexandria. Shirley and I were married at the beginning of my last year, and following ordination we began three wonderful years at St. Thomas's Church in Owings Mills, Maryland, where Henry and Em Rightor taught us something about parish ministry and how to survive as a clergy couple.

Years in Arlington, Virginia, as vicar of St. John's Mission Church included Katherine and Jennifer as well as the short life of our only son, Jonathan. There, as pretense and performance began to take their toll, my clerical collar began choking me, and I realized my questions and anxieties could no longer be denied or stilled. I continued saying things I neither understood nor believed but was convinced were true. Creedal orthodoxy proved a more bewildering maze than ever. I remained certain of but one thing—that those loving arms of God awaited me on the other side of finally growing up as I should, believing as I ought, and being a faithful priest, husband, and father. Back then I never imagined that it was a divine demon that tortured my quivering body during liturgy, haunted me with bizarre dreams and anguished night sweats, and even fueled me through endless squash games and long jogs. Preaching with some abandon about what little bit of church and Jesus I knew from experience to be true felt like my only reprieve.

In those days J. D. Salinger's *Catcher in the Rye* sat on best-seller lists, and his central character, Holden Caulfield, accused me of being "phoney." So I began searching the world for his little sister, because "when you told Phoebe something she knew exactly what the hell you were talking about." My Phoebe ended up being a Freudian analyst who saved my life by listening to me every morning for nearly three years. His arms were wide and welcoming, but not enough.

I spent twenty-five years in three wonderful congregations that sustained, nurtured, pampered, and even listened to me. Their hospitality and patience were both a sanctuary and a temporary hideout. At times I confused the everlasting arms I continued to seek with the church. As years passed, however, the armor loosened, resolves to be the perfect priest waned, pretending and performing no longer satisfied, and being good felt mostly hypocritical. David Whyte, the poet, tells of the assistant to Thomas Edison who bemoaned the wasted effort of a thousand failed attempts to find a successful light filament. "Ridiculous," Edison told him. "We now know a thousand ways it doesn't work!"[119] I discovered a thousand ways that priesthood, marriage, parenting, and just living with myself failed to work.

In 1983 Shirley and I went to Berkeley, California, where we regrouped. I got a graduate degree, and the Guild for Psychological Studies became an important part of our lives. Inspired by its founder, Elizabeth Boyden Howes, I no longer needed to pretend I believed that Jesus of Nazareth was only a creedal comma between "born of the Virgin Mary" and "crucified under Pontius Pilate." Instead, I met a Jesus whose life was central and whose death reflected the high cost of being present and true rather than performing and pretending. Emancipated from the role of example or savior, Jesus became instead a paradigm of what it means to be fully human. Hidden from me for most of my life beneath exegetical overlays and behind arcane theology of an orthodox Christ, this Jesus of the Gospels began finally to bridge the void between God's welcoming arms and me. With a liberated Jesus, Hebrew Scripture as well as Matthew, Mark, and Luke became my sacred story as well. Ancient drama with its cast of Bible characters began to describe my world and me.

Four years in Berkeley led to eight at the Educational Center in St. Louis, where I undertook a unique project to develop a biblical resource exploring a Jesus who revealed God in places outside the church, dependent on neither academia nor psychology. There, and later at Myers Park Baptist Church in Charlotte, North Carolina, I found that by living in the tension of Jesus' questions instead of prepackaged answers, I was exchanging an insatiable search for meaning in the Bible for the opportunity to read sacred narratives as life's drama around and within me. The goal was no longer to interpret the text; instead, it was to wonder how the story was happening in the world and also as an event in my life. To the degree that could and did happen for me, Jesus and I both came alive.

Myers Park Baptist Church was a Flannery O'Connor short story filled with beautiful people on a journey—more interested in life than in being doctrinally correct, right, or even righteous. Together we read between the lines and got hooked by the spaces and gaps of the Scripture stories where we found ourselves. Toward the end I was in Bible groups often several times a day, serving not so much as a leader or teacher as what Keats termed "a priest of the imagination."

The story began as a sleepy little boy on the swing carried through the dark safely to bed. The child who became a priest, and who is now a confessing elder, still searches and still experiences tension between living my truth and being present. I return to Jesus stories often, and each time I discover a different bent-over one or Samaritan or blind beggar or Jesus within and around me. Such moments are a revelation of God's presence and an epiphany of my own truth. Each time I realize I have met these people before and I am all of them at the same time. When Yogi Berra's famous line about "déjà vu all over again" happens in the Bible, the arms I have yearned for since forever are a bit closer. I am aware, as well, that whenever I can muster enough courage and risk the loving, I become the everlasting arms in the stories of those around me.

NOTES

1. Elaine Pagels, *Beyond Belief* (New York: Random House, 2003), 144.

2. Conventionally, a tension exists between *orthodoxy* (in literal Greek, "straight belief" or "upright opinion") and *heresy* (the Greek word for "choice") as right belief versus wrong belief. Bart Ehrman joins other scholars in pointing out "that the early church did not consist of a single orthodoxy from which emerged a variety of competing heretical minorities. Instead, earliest Christianity, as far back as we can trace our sources, could be found in a number of divergent forms, none of which represented the clear and powerful majority of believers against all the others." In some cases what was later considered heretical was an early form of Christianity. It was not until 381 at the Council of Constantinople convened by Emperor Theodosius that a revised version of the Nicene Creed was adopted defining what has subsequently become orthodox theology. Explore this little known but both important and intriguing theological adventure in *When Jesus Became God: The Epic Fight over Christ's Divinity in the Last Days of Rome* by Richard E. Rubenstein (New York: Harcourt Brace, 1999). The modern sense of both terms comes from the third and fourth centuries, when creeds were written as part of the emerging church.

3. Pagels, *Beyond Belief*, 145.

4. Alice Walker, *By the Light of My Father's Smile* (New York: Random House, 1998), 62–63.

5. From David Whyte, *Everything Is Waiting for You* (Langley, WA: Many Rivers Press, 2003), 4.

6. Trans. Leif Sjoberg and W. H. Auden (New York: Knopf, 1977), 89.

7. Kansas City: Andrews McNeel Publishing, 2001, 3.

8. DVD; Blue Wolf, Bungalow 78 Productions, Farrell/Minoff, 1998.

9. Carlsbad, CA: Hay House, 1999, 22–23.

10. From *Breathing the Water* (New York: New Directions Publishing, 1987).

11. New York: Plume (A Division of the Penguin Group), 1999, 215–16.

12. In *Dream Work* (New York: Atlantic Monthly Press, 1986), 38.

13. Paul Tillich, "You Are Accepted," in *The Shaking of the Foundations* (New York: Charles Scribner's Sons, 1948), chapter 19.

14. Andy Zubco, compiler, *Treasury of Spiritual Wisdom: A Collection of 10,000 Spiritual Quotes* (San Diego: Blue Dove, 1996), 446.

15. New York: Harcourt Brace Jovanovich, 1972, 663.

16. Dwight Goddard, ed., *A Buddhist Bible* (Boston: Beacon, 1994), 409.

17. Anchor Bay Entertainment, 1983.

18. New York: Charles Scribner, 1958, 113.

19. From *I Will Not Die an Unlived Life: Reclaiming Purpose and Passion* (Boston: Red Wheel/Weiser, 2000), 1.

20. Quoted in David Whyte, *The Heart Aroused* (New York: Doubleday, 1996), 96.

21. Harrisburg, PA: Morehouse Publishing, 1997, 57.

22. Mahwah, NJ: Paulist Press, 1986, 19.

23. Harrisburg, PA: Morehouse Publishing, 1997, 28.

24. Emeryville, CA: Shoemaker & Hoard Publishers, 2004, 39.

25. New York: HarperCollins, 2004, 140.

26. From *Daily Horoscope* (St. Paul, MN: Graywolf Press, 1986).

27. Trans. Anita Barrows and Joanna Macy (New York: Riverhead Books, 1996), 50.

28. David Whyte, "The Opening of Eyes" from *Songs for Coming Home* (Langley, WA: Many Rivers Press, 1999), 22.

29. New York: Harcourt Brace, 1952, 145.

30. Berkeley, CA: North Atlantic, 1990.

31. New York: W. W. Norton, 1994, 165.

32. Translated from the French quoted in Kathleen Rosenblatt, *René Daumal: The Life and Work of a Mystic Guide* (Albany, NY: Suny Press, 1999), 111.

33. From *Mechanical Birds* (Laurinburg, NC: St. Andrews College Press, 2000), 64. © Denver Butson. Reprinted with permission.

34. From *Picnic, Lightning* (Pittsburgh: University of Pittsburgh Press, 1998), 39–40. Permission requested.

35. From Sam Keen and Anne Valley-Fox, *Your Mythic Journey* (Los Angeles: Jeremy P. Tarcher, Inc., 1989), 48.

36. New York: Knopf, 1968, 22.

37. New York: Harper Paperbacks, 1996, 190–91.

38. San Francisco: Berrett-Koehler Publishers, 1999, 60.

39. St. Paul, MN: Graywolf Press, 2003, 27.

40. From *Selected Poems* (London: Faber and Faber Ltd, 1996).

41. From *Where the Sidewalk Ends* (New York: Harper & Row, 1974), 26.

42. Boston: Shambala, 1997, 9.

43. New York: Basic Books, 1999, 294.

44. New York: Penguin Books, 2002, 255–56.

45. New York: Marlowe & Co., 2001, 190.

46. New York: Riverhead Books, 2003, 164–65, 325–26.

47. From *The Complete Poems of D. H. Lawrence*, ed. V. de Sola Pinto and F. W. Roberts (New York: Viking Penguin, 1971), 50.

48. Joseph Telushkin, *Jewish Literacy: The Most Important Things to Know about the Jewish Religion, Its People and Its History* (New York: William Morrow, 2001), 734.

49. Ibid.

50. New York: Crossroad Classic, 1997.

51. Boston: Conari, 2000, 175.

52. New York: Marlowe & Co., 2001, 46.

53. Freedom, CA: The Crossing Press, 1984, 120–21.

54. Copyright © Elizabeth Cunningham. Reprinted with permission.

55. *The Kabir Book*, trans. Robert Bly (St. Paul: Beacon Press and Macmillan Press Ltd., 1993). Used by permission.

56. Ed. Rochard Aldington and Stanley Weintraub (New York: Penguin Books, 1946), 603.

57. New York: W. W. Norton, 2000, 156.

58. New York: Bantam, 1997, 128.

59. New York: Knopf, 2002, 54.

60. *The What It Is: New and Selected Poems* (St. Paul: Graywolf Press, 1998), 224.

61. *God Says Yes to Me* (Maine: Tilbury House Publishers, 1995), 6.

62. "The Teaching Co.: Great Figures of the New Testament, Part 1" (VHS; Chantilly, VA, 2002).

63. Ibid.

64. San Francisco: HarperSanFrancisco, 2004, 93.

65. New York: Columbia University Press, 1993, 167.

66. Orleans, MA: Paraclete Press, 2005, 3–5.

67. From Derek Walcott, *Collected Poems 1948–1984* (New York: Farrar, Straus and Giroux, 1986), 328.

68. Jared Diamond, *Collapse: How Societies Choose to Fail or Succeed* (New York: Viking, 2005), 275.

69. New York: Random House, 2002, 353.

70. Ed. Rochard Aldington and Stanley Weintraub (New York: Penguin Books, 1946), 586.

71. Boston: Shambhala, 2004, 166.

72. New York, Random House, 1961, 1989, 233–34.

73. From *Songs for Coming Home* (Langley, WA: Many Rivers Press, 1999), 22.

74. From *New and Selected Poems 1974–1994* (New York: W. W. Norton, 1994), 182.

75. From A. R. Ammons, *Bosh and Flapdoodle* (New York: W. W. Norton, 2005), 29.

76. Whyte, *Songs for Coming Home*, 22.

77. Ibid.

78. DVD; Touchstone Video, 1989, 1998.

79. New York: W. W. Norton, 1994, 285.

80. Used by permission.

81. New York: HarperCollins, 1998, 123.

82. www.painterskeys.com, editor Robert Genn.

83. New York: Vintage, 2000, 243.

84. New York: Picador USA, 1990, 318.

85. Quoted in John Dominic Crossan, *Jesus: A Revolutionary Biography* (New York: HarperCollins, 1994), 65.

86. New York: Harcourt, 1959, 11.

87. Albany, NY: SUNY Press, 1997, 105.

88. www.gardendigest.com.

89. Whitefish, MT: Kessinger, 2004, 16.

90. From *New Young American Poets*, ed. Kevin Prufer (Carbondale, IL: Southern Illinois University Press, 2000).

91. New York: Ballantine Books, 1999, 7.

92. From *The Poetry Anthology 1912–2002* (Chicago: Ivan R. Dee, 2002), 93. Used by permission.

93. In Shin Buddhism the ultimate goal of transformation comes in saying *nembutsu* (NAMA-AMIDA-BUTSU). It is the flowing call of the Buddha of Immeasurable Light and Life, coming from the fathomless center of life itself, as well as our response to that call without any hesitation or calculation.

94. William R. Evans III and Andrew Frothingham, *Crisp Toasts* (New York: St. Martin's Press, 1992), 43.

95. New York: Viking, 2004, 120.

96. New York: HarperSanFrancisco, 2005.

97. New York: Harcourt Brace Jovanovich, 1973, 214.

98. From *Where Many Rivers Meet* (Langley, WA: Many Rivers Press, 1996, 2004), 35.

99. Stephen Dunn, *New & Selected Poems* (New York: W. W. Norton, 1994), 33.

100. Used by permission of Thomas Moore.

101. Dallas: Spring Publications, 1975, 66.

102. www.thesunmagazine.org, September 11, 2001.

103. From *The Future*, Columbia/ATV songs, 1992.

104. New York: Harper & Row, 1976, 168.

105. From *Carnival Evening: New and Selected Poems 1968–1998* (New York: W. W. Norton, 1998), 262. Used by permission.

106. From *Passing Through: The Later Poems* (New York: W. W. Norton, 1995), 22. Used by permission.

107. From *The Collected Poems of Theodore Roethke* (New York: Anchor, 1975), 231.

108. "A Hard Death," in *Grace Confounding* (Minneapolis: Augsburg Fortress, 1972), 27.

109. Barbara Hurd, *Stirring the Mud* (New York: Houghton Mifflin, 2003), 109–10.

110. Harvey Cox, *When Jesus Came to Harvard* (New York: Houghton Mifflin, 2004), 38.

111. New York: Atheneum, 1977, 184.

112. New York: Penguin Press, 2004, 33.

113. Berkeley, CA: North Atlantic Books, 1990, 15.

114. London and New York: Fourth Estate, 2002, 1.

115. New York: Penguin Books, 1990, 165.

116. From *Days We Would Rather Know: Poems* (New York: Viking Press, 1984). Used by permission of Michael Blumenthal.

117. New York: Bantam, Doubleday, Dell, 1958, 5, 8.

118. New York: Alfred A. Knopf, 1988. Copyright © Paul Winston.

119. David Whyte, *The Heart Aroused: Poetry and the Preservation of the Soul in Corporate America* (New York, NY: Currency/Doubleday, 2002), 32.

FILMS: FINDING JESUS, DISCOVERING SELF IN THE REEL WORLD

Just as biblical texts, poems, and novels tell us stories that mirror our lives, so do motion pictures. Just because they never happened does not mean they are not true reflections of the choices and struggles that face us daily. Consider watching one of these films after engaging in and wondering about a Jesus event described in this book.

Begin by asking yourself the who, what, where, how, why, and when questions that we do.

- What is happening in the story?
- Who are the people, and what is going on between, around, and even inside of them?
- What kinds of questions haunt these people, and what decisions are they making or avoiding?
- Why are you so attracted to a particular character or situation?
- How does the film reflect what is happening in the world around you?
- Where do you meet the characters—on the evening TV news or in situation comedies, on the front page of your newspaper, on the bus to work or at the gym, in the next pew or at the grocery checkout counter?
- How do you know this story as an event in your personal life?
- When have you known the joys, struggles, and tears reflected in the film?
- How is the film happening in your office or classroom, around your dining room table, between you and people who matter most to you?
- How is the drama going on inside of you? Consider how all of the characters in the story may be alive and well in your psyche and soul.
- What links do you find between this film and the Jesus story with which you began?

- In what ways are the issues between the lines the same, and in what ways are they different?
- What do both the film and the Jesus story touch inside of you? How do they tilt your world by making you wonder about your assumptions?
- How do both of these stories urge you toward healing and the breath-taking promise of wholeness?

1. Leaving Home

Motorcycle Diaries chronicles Ernesto "Che" Guevara's decision to leave home, as he described in his journal by the same name: "I'm not the person I once was. All this wandering around 'our America with a capital *A*' has changed me more than I thought." During his perilous journey to mature adulthood, we watch the "spirit of a dreamer" experiencing an awakening. To leave or not to leave the familiar becomes for each of us a unique challenge confronted more than once. A challenge that implores us to risk waking up, tuning in, and listening to that restless and passionate one within who craves more for the world and self.

2. Beginning the Journey

Caught on a Train is a short (80-minute) BBC film starring Peggy Ashcroft, who as a prickly dowager challenges a young English businessman to wonder about the journey he is taking through life. The often-overcrowded compartment on the Ostend-Vienna express train invites us to look at the trip we are taking, no matter where we think we may be headed, through a new lens and from different perspectives.

3. Living with Wilderness

Julia, with Jane Fonda and Vanessa Redgrave, is based on Lillian Hellman's *Pentimento*. Here wilderness is a world on the brink of war as well as between two friends that raises issues around testing and temptation. Julia, who has devoted her life to fighting fascism in the 1930s, leads or drives Hellman into bewildering choices that finally she can neither escape nor deny.

4. Returning Home

I Never Sang for My Father stars Gene Hackman and Melvyn Douglas in the poignant story of a kindhearted son who devotes his life to winning the affection of his stubborn and opinionated father. At some level this haunting movie tells of the struggle of every child to break loose and every parent to let go. The ending is a critical reminder that lives end but relationships do not.

5. Weathering Storms

Touching the Void describes mountain climbers Joe Simpson and Simon Yates as they scale the never-before-conquered 21,000-foot Siula Grande in the Andes. It is true adventure filled with life-and-death choices. Simpson's decision to risk all by touching the void rather than opting for a safe and slow death will feel familiar to those who have ever faced such a moment of truth in a relationship, career, or meeting with self.

6. Speaking One's Truth

The Sea Inside is based on the life of Spaniard Ramon Sampedro, who fought a thirty-year campaign to win the right to end his life with dignity. The film is a joyful and heartrending experience that touches the sacred places in which death is a mirror of the deepest kind of living and loving. The German author Stifter writes, "Pain is a holy angel who shows treasures to men which otherwise remain forever hidden; through him men have become greater than through all joys of the world."

7. Loving with All

Frankie and Johnny, an R-rated film, opens with Frankie's bus trip across a bridge to attend a baptism as Johnny steps through prison doors that burst open to set him free. Al Pacino and Michelle Pfeiffer depict a unique love story that reflects how difficult it is for most of us to be vulnerable and available. As a coffee shop waitress and ex-con short-order cook, the two finally meet when scars that cannot be kissed away become the occasion for finding and loving one another. The healing story is timeless.

8. Standing Up Straight

Dead Poets Society is about John Keating (Robin Williams), who is central to young Neil's discovery of what he wants to do with his life "whether my father wants me to or not!" It is about *carpe diem*—"seize the day"—in the lives of teenage boys and their teacher, as well as in ours. The film pushes us to the edge of what is always a cost and promise of "seizing the day" or letting someone else define who we are.

9. Binding Wounds

In America is the poignant tale of a poor Irish family searching for a better life in America. Through the eyes of two little girls, we encounter their anguished parents. When confronted, at last, by painful scars deeply hidden and desperately held on to, the parents learn that sometimes it is the wounded and alien stranger who can point them toward healing and the promise of new life.

10. Crossing Boundaries

Vera Drake: Wife, Mother, Criminal showcases Imelda Staunton, one of the five nominees for the Best Actress Oscar in 2005 for her performance as Vera Drake, an Englishwoman living in the 1950s. Unbeknownst to her family, Vera secretly helps women terminate unwanted pregnancies. As her world unravels, the film poses hard but important questions about crossing boundaries to visit the "least of these" and the meaning of "healing." Dietrich Bonhoeffer wrote from prison in 1944 shortly before his death: "The experience that is a transformation of all human life is given in the fact that Jesus is there only for the others. Our relation to God is not a 'religious' relationship to the highest, most powerful, and best Being imaginable. . . . The transcendental is not infinite and unattainable tasks, but the neighbor who is within reach in any given situation."

11. Choosing Life

The Straight Story tells the true story of Alvin Straight, an elderly man with failing eyesight, who walks with two canes and rides his John Deere lawnmower 260 miles to visit his ill, alienated brother Lyle. Salman Rushdie writes, "The journey creates us. We become the frontiers we cross." Such an impending journey across life-defining frontiers awaits all of us. Sometimes it serves to take us farther and farther away and other times home to brother and self.

12. Discovering God's Kingdom

Ladies in Lavender features Judy Dench and Peggy Smith as sisters whose lives are on the way to transformation the morning a young man's body washes up on their beach along the Cornish coast. Mary Oliver writes, "To live in this world you must be able to do three things: to love what is mortal; to hold it against your bones knowing your own life depends upon it; and, when the time comes to let it go, to let it go." This film asks each of us how well we are able to do such things and where the world may be asking us to do them now.

13. Entering the Heart of the Matter

Shadowlands is a deeply moving love story about C. S. Lewis (Anthony Hopkins), the Oxford professor and famous writer, and Joy Gresham (Debra Winger), a feisty, abrasive New York Jewish divorcee and mother of a young son. The relationship calls into question the very foundations of Lewis's theology and his understanding of both the sacred and the all-too-human heart. As the film closes Lewis looks back: "I have been given the

choice twice in my life. The boy chose safety. The man chooses suffering."
It is the choice each of us makes to either live what Joy calls "the deal" or
reject and deny the pain and loss that happen at the center of an abun-
dant life.

14. Betraying Trust

Billy Elliot is a young boy from a working-class family who discovers a passion that will change his life. As an eleven-year-old rugged miner's son on
his way to boxing lessons, Billy stumbles into a ballet class. From that
moment on, a story about a boy's betrayal of the values of his blue-collar
family, as well as his father's ideals, begins to unfold. The film creates a
familiar tension between living our dreams and conforming to the hopes
of those who love us most, as it calls into question the role betrayal may
play as a part of growing up and building a loving relationship.

15. Epilogue: Breeding New Algebras

A River Runs Through It introduces us to a family in which "there was no
clear line between religion and fly-fishing." Robert Redford and Brad Pitt
relive the ancient tensions between brothers that, in the end, may be about
siblings found deep within each of us. The father of Norman asks his old-
est son, who has become a successful newspaperman, "You like to tell true
stories, don't you?" and he answers, "Yes, I like to tell stories that are true."
Then he asks him, "After you have finished your true stories sometime,
why don't you make up a story and the people to go with it? Only then will
you understand what happened and why. It is those we live with and love
and should know who elude us." After we at last tell the facts of our lives,
another story about what really happened may await us.

BIBLIOGRAPHY

Armstrong, Karen. *A History of God: The 4,000-Year Quest of Judaism, Christianity and Islam.* New York: Ballantine, 1993.

Bond, D. Stephenson. *Living Myth: Personal Meaning as a Way of Life.* Boston & London: Shambala, 1993.

Booker, Christopher. *The Seven Basic Plots: Why We Tell Stories.* New York: Continuum International Publishing Group, 2004.

Borg, Marcus J. *The God We Never Knew: Beyond Dogmatic Religion to a More Authentic Contemporary Faith.* New York: HarperCollins, 1997.

————. *Meeting Jesus Again for the First Time.* New York: HarperSanFrancisco, 1994.

————. *Reading the Bible Again for the First Time: Taking the Bible Seriously but Not Literally.* New York: HarperCollins, 2001.

Campbell, Joseph, with Bill Moyers. *The Power of Myth.* New York: Doubleday, 1988.

Crossan, John Dominic. *Jesus: A Revolutionary Biography.* New York: HarperSanFrancisco, 1994.

————. *Who Killed Jesus? Exposing the Roots of Anti-Semitism in the Gospel Story of the Death of Jesus.* New York: HarperCollins, 1998.

Crossan, John Dominic, and Jonathan L. Reed, *Excavating Jesus: Beneath the Stones, Behind the Texts.* New York: HarperCollins, 2001.

Dossey, Larry. *Healing Words: The Power of Prayer and the Practice of Medicine.* San Francisco: HarperSanFrancisco, 1993.

Ehrman, Bart D. *The New Testament: A Historical Introduction to the Early Christian Writings.* New York: Oxford University Press, 2004.

Friedman, Richard Elliot. *The Hidden Face of God.* New York: HarperCollins, 1995.

Funk, Robert W., Roy W. Hoover, and The Jesus Seminar, trans. and commentary. *The Five Gospels*. A Polebridge Publication. New York: Macmillan, 1993.

Herzog, William R., II. *Jesus, Justice, and the Reign of God: A Ministry of Liberation*. Louisville: Westminster John Knox Press, 2000.

———. *Parables as Subversive Speech: Jesus as Pedagogue of the Oppressed*. Philadelphia: Westminster John Knox Press, 1994.

———. *Prophet and Teacher: An Introduction to the Historical Jesus*. Louisville: Westminster John Knox Press, 2005.

Hillman, James. *Loose Ends*. Dallas: Spring Publications, 1983.

———. *The Soul's Code: In Search of Character and Calling*. New York: Random House, 1996.

Hollis, James. *The Archetypal Imagination*. College Station: Texas A&M University Press, 2000.

Horsley, Richard. *Jesus and the Spiral of Violence: Popular Jewish Resistance in Roman Palestine*. San Francisco: Harper & Row, 1987.

Horsley, Richard, and John S. Hanson. *Bandits, Prophets, and Messiahs: Popular Movements at the Time of Jesus*. Minneapolis: Winston Press, 1985.

Horsley, Richard, and James Tracy, ed. *Christmas Unwrapped: Consumerism, Christ, and Culture*. Harrisburg, PA: Trinity Press International, 2001.

Howes, Elizabeth Boyden. *Intersection and Beyond*. San Francisco: Guild for Psychological Studies Publishing House, 1971.

———. *Jesus' Answer to God*. San Francisco: Guild for Psychological Studies Publishing House, 1984.

Jesus Seminar, The. *The Once and Future Jesus*. Sonoma, CA: Polebridge Press, 2000.

Keen, Sam, and Anne Valley-Fox. *Your Mythic Journey: Finding Meaning in Your Life through Writing and Storytelling*. Los Angeles: Jeremy Tarcher, Inc., 1989.

Kegan, Robert. *In Over Our Heads: The Mental Demands of Modern Life*. Cambridge: Harvard University Press, 1994.

Keizer, Garret. *Help: The Original Human Dilemma*. San Francisco: HarperSanFrancisco, 2004.

King, Karen L. *The Gospel of Mary of Magdala: Jesus and the First Woman Apostle*. Santa Rosa, CA: Polebridge Press, 2003.

Klinghoffer, David. *Why the Jews Rejected Jesus*. New York: Random House, 2005.

Levine, Amy-Jill, ed. *A Feminist Companion to:* (14 volumes—specifically those on *Mark*, *Matthew*, and *Luke*). Cleveland, OH: Pilgrim Press, 2001.

Lifton, Robert J. *The Protean Self: Human Resilence in an Age of Fragmentation*. New York: Basic Books, 1993.

Maccoby, Hyman. *Judas Iscariot and the Myth of Jewish Evil*. New York: Free Press, 1992.

Miles, Jack. *God: A Biography*. New York: Alfred A. Knopf, 1995.

Moore, Thomas. *Care of the Soul*. New York: HarperCollins, 1992.

———. *Dark Nights of the Soul: A Guide to Finding Your Way through Life's Ordeals*. New York: Gotham Books, 2004.

———. *Original Self: Living with Paradox and Originality*. New York: HarperCollins, 2000.

Morrison, Mary C. *Approaching the Gospels Together*. Wallingford, PA: Pendle Hill Publications, 1986.

Myers, Ched. *Binding the Strong Man: A Political Reading of Mark's Story of Jesus*. Maryknoll, NY: Orbis Books, 1988.

Nelson-Pallmeyer, Jack. *Jesus against Christianity: Reclaiming the Missing Jesus*. Harrisburg, PA: Trinity Press International, 2001.

Ouaknin, Marc-Alain. *Symbols of Judaism*. Barnes & Noble, 2003.

Pagels, Elaine. *Beyond Belief: The Secret Gospel of Thomas*. New York: Random House, 2003.

———. *The Gnostic Gospels*. New York: Vintage Books, 1989.

Palmer, Parker. *The Courage to Teach: Exploring the Inner Landscape of a Teacher's Life*. San Francisco: Jossey-Bass, 1998.

Patterson, Stephen. *The God of Jesus: The Historical Jesus and the Search for Meaning*. Harrisburg, PA: Trinity Press International, 1998.

———. *The Gospel of Thomas and Jesus*. Sonoma, CA: Polebridge Press, 1993.

Phillips, Dorothy, Elizabeth Boyden Howes, and Lucille Nixon. *The Choice Is Always Ours*. San Francisco: Harper & Row, 1975.

Potok, Chaim. *Wanderings*. New York: Fawcett Crest, 1978.

Riches, John. *Jesus and the Transformation of Judaism*. New York: Seabury Press, 1982.

Sanford, John. *The Kingdom Within: The Inner Meaning of Jesus' Sayings*. San Francisco: HarperSanFrancisco, 1991.

Scott, Bernard Brandon. *Re-Imagine the World: An Introduction to the Parables of Jesus*. Santa Rosa, CA: Polebridge Press, 2001.

Sharman, Henry Burton. *Records of the Life of Jesus (Revised Standard Version)*. San Francisco: Guild for Psychological Studies Publishing House, 1991.

Silver, Abba Hillel. *Where Judaism Differs: An Inquiry into the Distinctiveness of Judaism*. New York: Macmillan, 1989.

Sinetar, Marsha. *Reel Power: Spiritual Growth through Film*. Liguori, MO: Triumph Books, 1993.

Spong, John Shelby. *Liberating the Gospels: Reading the Bible with Jewish Eyes*. New York: HarperSanFrancisco, 1996.

Steinberg, Rabbi Milton. *Basic Judaism*. New York: Harcourt Brace, 1975.

Steiner, George. *Real Presences*. Chicago: University of Chicago Press, 1989.

Telushkin, Rabbi Joseph. *Jewish Literacy: The Most Important Things to Know about the Jewish Religion, Its People, and Its History*. New York: William Morrow, 1991.

Throckmorton, Burton H., Jr. *Gospel Parallels: A Comparison of the Synoptic Gospels*. 5th ed. Nashville: Thomas Nelson, 1992.

VanNess, Patricia W. *Transforming Bible Study with Children: A Guide for Learning Together*. Nashville: Abingdon Press, 1991.

Vermes, Geza. *The Changing Faces of Jesus*. New York: Penguin Books, 2000.

Visotzky, Burton L. *Reading the Book: Making the Bible a Timeless Text*. New York: Anchor Books/Doubleday, 1991.

Wink, Walter. *The Bible in Human Transformation: Toward a New Paradigm for Biblical Study*. Philadelphia: Fortress Press, 1973.

———. *Engaging the Powers: Discernment and Resistance in a World of Domination*. Minneapolis: Fortress Press, 1992.

———. *The Human Being: Jesus and the Enigma of the Son of Man*. Minneapolis: Fortress Press, 2002.

———. *Transforming Bible Study: A Leader's Guide*. Nashville: Abingdon Press, 1980.

Documentary and Audio Media (Tapes and CDs)

Mystic Fire: www.mysticfire.com; 800–292–9001
New Dimensions: www.newdimensions.org; 800–925–8273
Public Broadcasting System: www.pbs.org
Sounds True: www.soundstrue.com; 800–333–9185
Speaking of Faith: www.speakingoffaith.org
The Teaching Company: www.TEACH12.com; 800–832–2412
Wisdom Radio: www.wisdomradio.com

Websites for Additional Insights

Beliefnet: www.beliefnet.com

The Bible Workbench: www.bibleworkbench.com

David Whyte, Many Rivers Company:
    http://davidwhyte.bigmindcatalyst.com

Explorefaith: www.explorefaith.org

Four Springs Seminars: www.foursprings.org

Guild for Psychological Studies: www.guildsf.org

Hollywood Jesus: http://www.hollywoodjesus.com/sixth_sense.htm

Journal of Religion and Film: http://www.unomaha.edu/jrf/

My Jewish Learning: www.myjewishlearning.com

On a Journey: www.onajourney.org

Speaking of Faith: www.speakingoffaith.org

Spiritual Cinema Circle: www.spiritualcinemacircle.com

Spirituality and Health: www.spiritualityhealth.com

PERMISSIONS

INDEX

*Abounding Grace: An Anthology
of Wisdom* (Peck), 4
Abraham, 115–16
   daughter of, 54, 58
adultery, 112
Age of Iron (Coetzee), 118
algebra, new, 112–19
Amazing Grace, 9
Ammons, A. R., 78
*Anam Cara: A Book of Celtic
Wisdom* (O'Donohue), 85
Angelou, Maya, 59
angels, 15
anointment, of prophets, priests,
   and kings, 27
archetype, xv
Ark of the Covenant, 11
Assyrians, 64
audio media, 142
Awakening the Fire Within
   (Dols), ix

Babylon, 11, 28
Bambaren, Sergio, 5
baptism
   as beginning, 12
   of Jesus, 8, 18
   purposes of, 10

Bartimaeus, 80, 82, 83
Being, voice of, 121
Berra, Yogi, 128
Berry, Wendell, 22
Bethphage, 96
betrayal
   by Judas Iscariot, 103, 106–8
   of women and children, 104–6
Beyond Belief (Pagels), xvi
Bible, xv
The Bible Workbench, viii, ix
Billy Elliot, 137
"Bits of Rubble Turn into Gold"
   (Tz'u-min), 95
Black Mustard, 90–91
blindness, Jesus' healing of, 80
"block busters," 26
"Blue in Green (for Chris)"
   (Butson), 30
Blumenthal, Michael, 119
Bly, Robert, 48
boatlift, Cuban, 68
"The Book" (Pastan), 109
Book of Hours: Love Poems to God
   (Rilke), 24
bread, from stones, 19
"Breakage" (Oliver), 54
Buber, Martin, 12

Buddha, 38, 95, 115–16
    of Immeasurable Light and Life,
        132n. 93
Buddhism, 38–39, 114
    Shin, 132n. 93
Bullitt-Jonas, Margaret, 85
Butson, Denver, 30
By the Light of My Father's Smile
    (Walker), xvi

Caesar
    Empire of, 99
    as Savior, 99
Care of the Soul (Moore), xi
Catcher in the Rye (Salinger), 127
Catskills, 87
Caught on a Train, 134
Chanukah, 122
Chardin, Pierre Teilhard de, 12
Chevalier, Tracy, 5
Chodrön, Pema, 38, 76
"The Clay Jug" (Kabir), 53
Cleveland Jewish News, viii
Cleveland Plain Dealer, viii
The Clothesline Project, 104
Coetzee, J. M., 118
Collapse (Diamond), 72
The Collected Poems (Kunitz), 59
Collins, Billy, 30
"A Color of the Sky" (Hoagland), 37
*The Columbia Dictionary of
    Quotations* (Kundera), 67
"Come to the Edge" (Logue), 37
Commandments, Ten, 11, 112
Common Era, xiv
compassion, 64
Complete Poems 1913–1962
    (cummings), 11
The Complete Poems and Plays
    (Eliot), 29
*A Continuous Harmony: Essays
    Cultural and Agricultural*
    (Berry), 22

Coping, viii
The Cornel West Reader (West), 44
The Courage to Teach (Palmer), ix
Covenant, Ark of the, 11
Cox, Harvey, 117
crisis, as opportunity, 18
Cuban boatlift, 68
cummings, e. e., 11
Cunningham, Elizabeth, 52
Cunningham, Michael, 86

Dead Poets Society (Keating), 84, 135
Descartes, 41
desert, 21–22
The Desert: An Anthology for Lent
    (Moses), 21–22
Deuteronomy, 49
    22:9   91
devil. *See also* Satan
    temptations by, 15
Diamond, Jared, 72
disciples, of Jesus, 35
disease, nature of, 41
documentaries, 142
The Dolphin: The Story of a Dreamer
    (Bambaren), 5
donkey, 96
D'Souza, Alfred, 85
Dunn, Stephen, 29, 77, 85, 101

Easter, 115
Edison, Thomas, 127
Egypt, xv, 113
Ehrman, Bart, 129n. 2
Eliade, Mircea, 93
Elijah, 26
Eliot, T. S., 29
Elisha, 26
Emerson, Ralph Waldo, 59, 89
Empire of God, 91
Episcopal Church, 123
eternal truths, xvi
Evensong (Godwin), 94

Evolution and Ethics (Huxley), 93
Exodus, 11

faith, lack of, 36
fasting, 15
father, honoring of, 112
fear, 36
Fearing, Kenneth, 82
films, 133–37
Finding Mañana: A Memoir of a Cuban Exodus (Ojito), 68
forgiveness, of sin, 10
Forward Day-By-Day, viii
Foster, Ruth S., 93
Frankie and Johnny, 135

Galilee
   Jesus' return to, 25
   Jubilee Year in, 28
Garofalo, Michael, 93
The Gift of Truth: Gathering the Good (Ross), 93
Gioia, Dana, 23
Girl With A Pearl Earring (Chevalier), 5
glacier, 22
God
   Caesar as Son of, 99
   Empire of, 91
   goodness of, 112
   kingdom of, 87, 112
   law of, 57
   love for, 47–51
   as One, 50
"God Says Yes To Me" (Haught), 60
God's Politics: Why the Right Gets It Wrong and the Left Doesn't Get It (Wallis), 101
Godwin, Gail, 94
Goffin, Gerry, 86
Goldman, Caren, 52, 68
good-bye, 1–2
Good Samaritan, 64

gospel. *See also* John; Luke; Mark; Matthew; Thomas
   as chapter and verse, 18
grace, 9–10
Greenland, 72
Guevara, Ernesto "Che," 134
Guild for Psychological Studies, 127
Gulag Archipelago 1918–1956 (Solzhenitsyn), 109

Hammarskjöld, Dag, 4
Hanukah, 8
"A Hard Death" (Wilder), 113
Haught, Kaylin, 60
Havel, Vaclav, 121
healing
   higher power for, 9
   by Jesus, 40, 54, 70, 80
   nature of, 98
"Healing" (Lawrence), 46
Healing Words for the Body, Mind and Spirit (Goldman), viii, 52
"Heart Prayer" (Cunningham), 52
heaven, treasure in, 112
Hebrew Scripture, 127
hello, 1–2
Help (Keizer), 67
Helprin, Mark, 118
hemorrhages, woman with, 40
heresy, xvi, 129n. 2
higher power, for healing and wholeness, 9
Hillel the Elder, 17
Hillman, James, 108–9
Hill, Twainhart, 85
Hoagland, Tony, 37
Ho Chi Minh, 68
Holocaust, 121–22
Holy Hunger: A Woman's Journey from Food Addiction to Spiritual Fulfillment (Bullitt-Jonas), 85
Holy of Holies, 11
Homan, Daniel, 67

A Home at the End of the World
    (Cunningham), 86
Homeland Security, 98
hometown, leaving from, 3
Hosseini, Khaled, 45
Hours of Gold, Hours of Lead:
    Diaries and Lectures 1929–1973
    (Lindbergh), 101
Howell, Mike, 68–69
Hurde, Barbara, 116
Huxley, Thomas Henry, 93
hypocrites, 54

I and Thou (Buber), 13
"I Go Back to the House for a Book"
    (Collins), 30
I Know Why the Caged Bird Sings
    (Angelou), 59
"In a Dark Time" (Roethke), 111
In America, 135
I Never Sang for My Father, 134
Inferno (Dante), 63
infirmity
    of spirit, 57
"Insomnia" (Gioia), 23
Intuition, viii
"In View of the Fact" (Ammons), 78
Iona (Scotland), 41
Irenaeus, xvi
Isaiah, 25
    visions of, 28
Israel, kingdom of, 64
"It Is I Who Must Begin"
    (Havel), 121
"It's Nice to Know What You're
    Doing," 3
"I Will Not Die an Unlived Life"
    (Markova), 12, 52

Jericho, 80, 82, 83
Jerusalem
    Jesus entering into, 96, 99
    Temple of, 11, 20, 64

Jesus
    baptism of, 8, 18
    betrayal of, 103–8
    birth of, meanings of, xvi
    blindness healed by, 80
    calming wind storm, 33
    crucifixion of, 115
    disciples of, 35
    in Galilee, 25
    healing by, 40, 54, 70, 80
    Jerusalem entered by, 96, 99
    as Jew, xiv, 124
    lawyer's answer from, 47, 49
    laying hands by, 54
    Nazareth left by, 3
    power of spirit and, 25
    resurrection of, 115
    Satan's rejection by, 20
    as Son of David, 83, 96
    temptations of, 19–20
    in wilderness, 15
    in wind storm, 33
Jews
    Hanukah and, 8
    Passover and, 122
    Rosh Hashonah and, 121
    synagogue and, 28, 54, 63
    The Talmud and, 67
    Torah and, 99
    tribes of, 64
John, 106
John Paul II, 44
John the Baptist, 1
Jordan River, 19
"The Journey" (Oliver), 6
Jubilee Sabbath of Sabbaths, 27, 28
Judah, kingdom of, 64
Judaism, 64, 124
Judas Iscariot, 103, 106–8
Judea, 64
Julia, 134
Just Because It Didn't Happen (Dols), ix
Juster, Norton, 76

Kabir, 53
karma, 95
Keating, John, 84
Keizer, Garrett, 67
Kidd, Sue Monk, 44
The Kite Runner (Hosseini), 45
Kundera, Milan, 67
Kunitz, Stanley, 59, 110

Ladies in Lavender, 136
Lao-tzu, 11
"La Poesia" (Neruda), 13
Lawrence, D. H., 46
lawyer, with Jesus, 47, 49
Leadership and the New Science
    (Wheatly), 37
Let Your Life Speak (Palmer), ix
Levertov, Denise, 5
Levine, Amy-Jill, 64
Leviticus 19:19   91
Lewis, C. S., 136
Lindbergh, Anne Morrow, 101
"Listen to the Mustn'ts"
    (Silverstein), 38
Livingston, Gordon, 71
Logue, Christopher, 37
"Long Live The Weeds"
    (Roethke), 94
"Long Term" (Dunn), 101
Loose Ends (Hillman), 108–9
Lord. *See* God
Lorde, Audre, 52
"Love After Love"
    (Walcott), 69
love, of God, 47–51
"Loves" (Dunn), 85
Lucifer. *See also* Satan
    as light giver, 21
Luke, xix, 19, 28, 106, 113, 123
    4:14–30   25–26
    10:25–28   47
    10:30–35   61
    13:10–17   54

MacIntyre, Alasdair, 117
"A Man Lost By A River"
    (Blumenthal), 119
Marines, 98
Mark, xix, 11, 90, 106, 113, 123
    1:9   1
    1:9–11   8
    4:30–32   87
    4:35–41   33
    5:24–34   40
    10:17–22   112
    10:46–52   80
    14:10–11   103
    14:43–46   103
    16:1–8   114
Markings (Hammarskjöld), 4
Markova, Dawna, 12, 52
Mary Magdalene, 115
Masser, Michael, 86
Matthew, xix, 19, 106, 113, 123
    4:1–11   15
    15:21–29   70
    21:1–13   96
The Measure of My Days (Scott-
    Maxwell), 37
Mencken, H. L., 37
Minot, Susan, 59
Mohamed, 115–16
money changers, 96
Montaigne, Michel de, 100
Moore, Thomas, xi, 108
Moses, xiv, 115–16
    books of, 64
    as prince of Egypt, xv
    scripture by, 19
    vision of, 27
Moses, John, 21–22
mother, honoring of, 112
Motorcycle Diaries, 134
"The Mound Builders" (Kunitz), 59
Mount Gerizim, 64
Mount of Olives, 96
Mt. Freedom (New Jersey), 87–90

murder, 112
music, xx
Mustard, Black, 90–91
mystery, 11
myths, 118

Naaman the Syrian, 26
Nag Hammadi (Egypt), 113
narcissism, xi, 62, 110
Natural Health, viii
Nazareth
    Jesus leaving, 3
    symbolism of, 3–4
Neruda, Pablo, 12
New Age Journal, viii
New And Selected Poems 1974–1994
    (Dunn), 29, 85
9/11, 35, 101, 112–13
Norsemen, 72

Oasis Gardens, 97
OB. *See* Outward Bound
O'Brien, Tim, xiv
Ode to My Father (Hill), 85
O'Donohue, John, 85
Ojito, Mirta, 68
Old Testament, xv
Oliver, Mary, 6, 54
"ONE: The Portrait" (Kunitz), 110
"The Opening of Eyes" (Whyte),
    76, 81
*Ordinary People As Monks and
    Mystics: Lifestyles for Self
    Discovery* (Sinetar), 22
orthodoxy, 129n. 2
Outward Bound (OB), 15–18, 123

The Pacific and Other Stories
    (Helprin), 118
Pagels, Elaine, xvi
Palmer, Parker, ix
"Parable Of The Fictionist"
    (Dunn), 77

Passover, 122
Pastan, Linda, 109
Patch Adams, 5
Pax Dei, 99
Pax Romana, 99
Peck, M. Scott, 4
The Phantom Tollbooth (Juster), 76
pity, 64
Pliny the Elder, 90–91
Pontius Pilate, 127
Pope John Paul II, 44
The Portable Oscar Wilde, 59, 76
Price, Reynolds, 117
The Prince of Egypt, xiv
Promised Land, 10, 62
Psalm 91:11–12   20
"Purple Loosestrife"
    (Townsend), 93
Pythagoras, 91

Quest for the Grail (Rohr), 51

Radical Hospitality (Homan), 68
Rapture (Minot), 59
Reflection, xix–xx
*René Daumal: The Life and
    Work of a Mystic Guide*
    (Rosenblatt), 29
repentance, 10
*A Return to Love: Reflections on
    the Principles of "A Course in
    Miracles"* (Williamson), 37
right, v. wrong, xix
Rilke, Ranier Maria, 24, 118
Ringe, Sharon, 28
A River Runs Through It, 137
Roethke, Theodore, 94, 111
Rohr, Richard, 51
Roman Empire, 19
Rosenblatt, Kathleen, 29
Rosh Hashonah, 121
Ross, Stephen, 93
Rushdie, Salman, 76

Sabbath, 54
  observance of, 63
The Sacred and Profane: The Nature
  of Religion (Eliade), 93
Salinger, J. D., 127
samara, 38
Samaria, destruction of, 64
Samaritan, Good, 61, 64
Sampedro, Ramon, 135
Satan, 54. *See also* devil; Lucifer
  Jesus' rejection of, 20
  as light bringer, 21
  temptations of, 15
Scott-Maxwell, Florida, 37
The Sea Inside, 135
The Secret Life of Bees (Kidd), 44
"Seeds" (Garofalo), 93
Shabbot, 63
Shadowlands, 136
shadow side, 48
shamans, 41
shame, 64
Shelley, Mary Wollstonecraft, 109
Shields, Carol, 118
Shin Buddhism, 132n. 93
Sh'ma, 47–51
"The Shonderosa," 89
shul, 114, 116
Sidon, 70
Silverstein, Shel, 38
Simpson, Joe, 22, 135
Sinetar, Marsha, 22
sin, forgiveness of, 10
Sister Outsider: Essays and Speeches
  (Lorde), 52
Smith College, 103
Solomon, 11
Solzhenitsyn, Aleksandr Isaevich, 109
"Sometimes" (Whyte), xxii
"soul loss," 41
spirit
  of infirmity, 57
  of Jesus, 25

  of the Lord, 27
  power of, 28
Spirituality and Health, viii
Stafford, William, 59
Start Where You Are: A Guide
  to Compassionate Living
  (Chodrön), 76
Stein, Gertrude, 71
Step Across the Line: Collected
  Nonfiction 1992–2002
  (Rushdie), 75
stones, into bread, 19
The Straight Story, 136
suffering, inevitability of, 38
suicide, 40
Sunbeams: A Book of Quotations
  (Syfransky), 29, 118
Syfransky, Sy, 29, 118
synagogue, 28, 54, 63

Tabernacle, 11
The Talmud, 67
Tarot, xvi
taxes, to Romans, 19
Telushkin, Joseph, 50
temptations
  of Jesus, 19–20
  by Satan, 15
Ten Commandments, 11, 112
Tender Mercies, 11
"Theme from Mahogany" (Masser and
  Goffin), 86
Thomas, 113
  97   112
Thoreau, Henry David, 3, 84
Three Dimensional Man (Dols), ix
Tillich, Paul, 10
tithes, to Romans, 19
Toklas, Alice, 71
Too Soon Old, Too Late Smart
  (Livingston), 71
Torah, 99
Touching the Void, 22, 135

Townsend, Ann, 93
Trevor, William, 100
tribes, Jewish, 64
truth
    as drug, 45
    eternal, xvi
    inner, 51
    quest for, 44
    speaking, 115
    whole, 43
"Turn Over Your Hand" (Stafford), 59
Twin Towers, 112
Tyre, 70
Tz'u-min, 95

Unless (Shields), 118

"Variation on a Theme by Rilke"
    (Levertov), 5
The Velveteen Rabbit (Williams), 119
Vera Drake: Wife, Mother, Criminal,
    136
Vietnam war, 68
    deaths in, 104
Virgin Mary, 127
Vitality and Wellness: An Omega
    Institute Mind, Body, Spirit Book
    (Goldman), viii
voice, of Being, 121
Voorhees, Ted, 123–24

Walcott, Derek, 69
Walker, Alice, xvi
Wallis, Jim, 101
websites, 143

Weight Watchers, 81
"The Well of Grief" (Whyte), 101
West, Cornel, 44
What Narcissism Means to Me
    (Hoagland), 37
Wheatly, Margaret, 37
When Things Fall Apart
    (Chodrön), 38
Whole New Life: An Illness and
    A Healing (Price), 117
whole truth, 43
Whyte, David, xix, xxii, 27, 76, 81,
    101, 127
Wilde, Oscar, 59, 76
Wilder, Amos, 113
wilderness, 15–24
Williams, Margery, 119
Williamson, Marianne, 37
Williams, William Carlos, xx
wind storm, and Jesus, 33
The Wizard of Oz, 99
Wojtyla, Karol (Pope John Paul II), 44
Wolfe, Thomas, 1
"Words Never Worked," 31
wrong, v. right, xix

Yates, Simon, 135
Yiddish, 114
Yoga Journal, viii
Yom Kippur, 121
"You Are Accepted," 10
Your Mythic Journey, 31

zero, 112, 117
Zion, daughter of, 96